The Healing Energy of Love

For Klazina,
Bonded together in
Love

John Allan

QUEST BOOKS
are published by
The Theosophical Society in America,
a branch of a world organization
dedicated to the promotion of brotherhood and
the encouragement of the study of religion,
philosophy, and science, to the end that man may
better understand himself and his place in
the universe. The Society stands for complete
freedom of individual search and belief.
In the Theosophical Classics Series
well-known occult works are made
available in popular editions.

All photographs by Letitia Allan

The Healing
Energy of Love

A Personal Journal *by John Allan*

Foreword by Kenneth Ring
author of "Heading Toward Omega"

*This publication made possible with
the assistance of the Kern Foundation*

The Theosophical Publishing House
Wheaton, Ill. U.S.A.
Madras, India / London, England

The Theosophical Publishing House
306 West Geneva Road
Wheaton, Illinois 60189

A publication of the Theosophical Publishing House, a
department of the Theosophical Society in America.

Library of Congress Cataloging in Publication Data.

Allan, John
  The healing energy of love.

  "A Quest original"—T.p. verso.
  1. Allan, John.   2. Psychical research—
Biography. 3. Healers—United States—Biography.
I. Title.
BF1027.A49A53   1986   299'.93   85-40770
ISBN 0-8356-0603-1 (pbk.)

CONTENTS

FOREWORD

BY KENNETH RING, PH.D.

My curiosity about John Allan was first aroused several years ago when he wrote me a beautiful letter concerned with my study of near-death experiences. In his letter John asked me whether I agreed with him that the feeling of beauty, peace and unconditional love that many near-death experiencers report suffuse them while they are on the threshold of (apparently imminent) death could be a common experience of the living. When I emphatically replied that I did—and, moreover, that this was an extremely important insight that many persons familiar with near-death experiences had overlooked—a friendship was born between us.

That friendship blossomed in further correspondence and, as it did so, my interest in John and his personal understanding of what he called "Spirit" continued to increase. Finally, in the summer of 1982 I traveled to California to spend some time with John, his wife, Letitia, as well as a close friend and collaborator of the Allans, Caroline Terrell. It was there, over a period of two weeks, that our ripening friendship culminated in John's sharing with me the fruits of his journey in and with Spirit. It is that same journey—or, rather, a continuation of it—that John will share with you in this book.

Before I tell you something more about what you will find in this book, however, let me say just a bit about John himself. I think if you form something of a mental picture of the author, his words, already powerful, will be likely to penetrate even more deeply into you. Toward that end, then, a few impressions of John and the environment in which he works.

John Allan is a big man—about six foot five, I'd say. His manner—and his being—exudes love in abundance. John doesn't shake hands, he hugs. And there is nothing tepid about his hugs: you *feel* his loving warmth radiating through you when he embraces you. Though John has spent much time by himself, when in company he talks animatedly, using his hands freely and expansively to emphasize the points he is making. His speaking (and singing) voice is a beautifully resonate baritone, as a result of which his speech is not only a stimulant to the mind but an esthetic delight to the ear. When John speaks with greatest conviction and obvious wisdom, it is when he dwells on (and, I believe, in) Spirit. When I read the words in this book about the nature of Spirit, I hear John's velvet voice in my mind. Maybe, to a degree, you will too.

John lives in a gorgeous section of California, right on the ocean and not far from some very appealing foothills where many of his excursions into Spirit have taken place. As you will be able to tell from reading this book, John is drawn to solitary explorations of the ranch lands and shoreline of this locale because such settings are likely to be conducive to the energies of Spirit. Many of the reflections you will find in this book originated in these places of immense beauty and power.

In my visits with John and his collaborators in this work of Spirit, I have walked and meditated where he has spent so much time; I have enjoyed many rich hours of conversational exchange and not a few of silent communing; and I have seen John interact with his wife, children, colleagues, and friends. What I have *experienced* with John has been only love, the kind of love that comes from direct contact with and knowledge of Spirit. John does not simply write about what is dear to him; he is an exemplar of it.

So, then, what of this "Spirit" of which John speaks so splendidly? Just what does John mean by this word, and why does it inform every page of this book?

To understand John's usage of Spirit—as well as the uses of Spirit—it is first necessary to appreciate that Spirit is an *energy*; one can *feel* Spirit. But more than that: Spirit is Life itself, the Life that lies beyond and outside of the world of matter; it is, in a phrase, Eternal Life.

John writes from a personal experience of life that confirms for him the basic *dualism* of the world into which we are born. Though variants of this point of view can be found in ancient Zoroasterianism, in the early Gnostics of the first century, and in the Cathars of the twelfth century, it is important to stress here that John comes to this understanding largely out of his own experience of Spirit—an experience which you, the reader, are invited and encouraged to verify for yourself.

From the standpoint of Spirit, then, the material world is akin to a dream—a waking dream maintained by the senses which function mechanically, devoid of Spirit. Yet, as the senses plunge us into the dream, this world seems real enough, and though it affords us experiences of beauty and pleasure, it is also the source of all our pain, suffering, horror, decay and, finally, death. As some of John's commentaries suggest, however, when the senses obscure Spirit, the world of matter *appears* to be one in which God has no commerce and had no creative role; here He is truly *Deus Absconditus*. The world of Spirit, on the other hand, stands entirely apart from the world of matter and is in every respect at antipodes to it. This is God's world, and it can be ours if we will but learn to open ourselves to the energy which is Spirit. The contrasts between and the ultimate irreconcilability of these two worlds are made clear in many of the entries in this book. For example:

"Where this material world is bound by time and space, the World of Love is eternal and infinite. Where this world's substance is matter, Love's World's substance is Spirit. Where this world is plagued by sickness, accidents, and death, Love's World is absolute wholeness, harmony, and eternal life."

And again:

"You close your eyes, let go of all material sensations, and enter that vast infinitude where Spirit abides. Here, there are no disharmonies; no time, no sorrow, no pain, no fear, no death. Here all is perfect and at peace. To live here eternally with Eternity while one is still on earth is the challenge and the work."

"You open your eyes and see imperfection and limitations all about; everything—the ocean, the houses, the birds, the people—speaks of temporality. And in these things is disharmony, pain, and suffering. It must be so, for deeply all these things of time and matter are unreal; they are illusory for only the eternity of Spirit is real."

The aim of this book—which takes the form of John's diary entries over the course of a year—is to show you how it is possible to escape from the confines of the world of matter and open yourself to the profound and timeless Love of the world of Spirit. To do this is to *live* in that world in the course of your daily life.

Still, do not make the mistake of thinking that this book is written mainly to "inspire" or to indulge in grandiloquent spiritual discourse or, worse yet, to exhort you to some sort of "self-improvement." It is and does none of these things. It is a supremely *practical* book which, among other things, will make clear how illness is caused and how you, like the author, can heal yourself. It also deals with such issues as overcoming grief and conquering the fear of death. Furthermore, it enables you to see what keeps you from feeling the joy that is *inherent* in life and from experiencing the love that is everyone's birthright. These and many other problems in living (and dying) yield to the overwhelming presence of Spirit. In this book John Allan, in prose as pellucid as the mountain streams he frequents, beckons you to follow him into the world of Spirit and to learn for yourself how Spirit works—and how it can work for you.

Can any of us afford not take this journey at some time in our life?

You are fortunate to have a guide like John Allan to help illuminate your way.

So was I.

PREFACE

I first started writing a journal in 1967. This was a period of my life when I was living alone. During this time, I was doing a considerable amount of reading, writing and experimenting. The experiments focused on trying to be constantly aware of what was happening both inside and outside myself, on trying to look at all of life—nature, people, myself—simply, without any judgment, on trying to quiet the mind to discover what lay behind and beyond thought.

Since many times these experiments brought on deep experiences of a different energy—a joyous, loving, and healing energy—I began quite naturally to write about them. I discovered that these records helped me immeasurably, especially when I was feeling troubled. I would often go to the journals and reread how I had previously come through similar problems. This would usually lift me off the plane of mulling, the place where problems often put one, and get me back into feeling life again; and increasingly I was becoming convinced that this, the life lived with Spirit's energy, is the only real life that there is.

In 1981, after completing *Conversations in Spirit,** I began considering what form my writing would now take. As I waited to see, I began reading personal journals of several authors. For years I've enjoyed reading books of this kind because I learn from them in much the same way that I learn from each person I know. This is why, I believe, one day the thought struck me: Why not write a journal? It's such a natural form for me. Also, a journal would offer the reader more of a behind-the-scenes look at the energy of Spirit and how one experiences it, heals with it, and lives with it daily, despite the many problems which arise. It might even encourage others to seek ways to live this way themselves.

So in April of 1983 I began recording events just as they occurred. I never dreamt I'd be recording my son's death, nor had I any idea what I would write. I did know I wanted the writing to represent, as honestly as possible, what this life of Spirit is about on a daily basis. Thus it had to be more experiential than philosophical. Though I do attempt, at times, to analyze the meaning of an experience, particularly after being with Spirit deeply, I've tried to keep this to a minimum, for I don't think anyone can definitely know fully what is happening. And that's one of the beauties of living with Spirit—it's a mystery which contains that magic of joy and love.

---

*John Allan, Letitia Allan, Caroline Terrell, (Marina Del Rey, CA: Devorss & Co., 1981).

JOURNAL ENTRIES

Monday, April 11, 1983

I drove inland this morning and found a beautiful broad
expanse of rolling meadows with pine trees all about.
Off in the distance were the mountains, green from the
winter rains. The sky was luminous, filled with billowy
white clouds in the west and in the north, while in the
east thunderheads were forming which foretold of a
coming storm.

What a joy it is to walk in wide open spaces. It seems
to help clear the mind and open the heart to the beauty
that's all around. And if perchance one is feeling a depth
of love, then this is ecstasy.

It was like that this morning. The energy of love was
within and without and all around. I could feel it, see it,
almost taste the deliciousness of the love which contained all within it. I wish at these times that everyone
in the world could feel this sense of beauty and love
pulsating from every pore of the earth and sky, from the
body and air. If we could just touch upon the energy of
love several times each day, then our lives would be
greatly enriched. And if we pursued the energy—if we
sought it with all our hearts—then what might our lives
become? Surely this energy, this life of love, is what

1

we've all been searching for. And to find it, which is to feel it, is to realize our life's fulfillment.

To become naked and innocent as a newborn babe, this is how one can experience that energy of love which comes from Spirit. Such words, I know, are only indicators and arise after the fact of feeling the energy. Then one looks from that state and describes the naked innocence of the love which is the substance of the energy.

How does one get to that place of nakedness and innocence? Surely one way is to drop all remembrances—all one's past and present thoughts and feelings; to drop all previous identifications with one's self and one's surroundings. Then from that place of unremembering we can look afresh at the life which is all around. And when we do we'll find that we're looking from a purity, we're looking from an untouchedness which is part of this life of love. Now there's the simple act of seeing without the self clouding up one's sight. This state of being is ultimate nakedness, ultimate innocence. This state of being is pure joy, ecstatic love.

As I was walking this morning along a path on a palisade overlooking the ocean, I realized that I was looking out from self, out from the ego, out from a mind filled with many thoughts.

After a while I sat down on a bluff overlooking a small cove. For a few more minutes I continued to look out from my head, to look out from the haze of the ego

and a tired body. Then wishing to reverse this process, wishing to come alive again, I exploded outwards: I mentally shifted, I mentally jumped, I transferred from being and observing from inside myself to being and observing from outside myself.

Now there was a complete loss of self-focus. Now I was actually down with the rocks below, down with the sand and the water and that small shore bird. I was now part of everything I saw, part of everything I heard: part of the sea, of the gulls flying overhead, of the otter playing on its back on top of the waves. I was also part of the sound of the ocean crashing over the dark rocks. Through the transferring of attention and energy and sight and hearing and feeling from myself to those things all about, I was released from living only within the mind and body, and I came awake again. With this awakening, my whole mind and being were filled with an energy, a drive, a renewed passion for life.

3

It sometimes feels that located in the place where the body is, is the true spiritual being of the individual. Here the person is pure, a part of Spirit and untouched by the evil of the world. In this place the person lives without sickness, without fear, without death; we live in total beingness without a blemish.

Now enter the body's speakings, complaints, and material feelings. Now we have the ending of the pure person's Nirvana—his Heaven. Now that pure person who really is untouched by every form of evil begins to think in terms of the body, in terms of matter. Thus enters fear. And from fear, conditioning. And from conditioning, material laws about the body which the person must abide by; otherwise the body's verdict will be ill health and possible death. So from Eden we descend into Hell to live there until the cloak of materiality—the body—is either overcome through transcendence or shucked off through death.

Saturday, April 16

The shore birds were everywhere, groveling along in the sand, searching for sand crabs and other things to eat. In the water among the rocks were cormorants and oyster catchers searching for fish they could breakfast on. One of the cormorants kept ducking its head under the water, evidently to make sure there was a fish awaiting before making its dive. Seagulls floated overhead, craning their necks looking for something to eat. And off in the distance close to the horizon were two freighters lazying their way across the waves toward some distant port. Truly the day was magical, filled with beauty and teeming with life.

Our friend said to us that if she had an ocean view

like this she would be totally contented. "Yes," I commented, "but I find I must see things anew, otherwise even this incredible view can become old hat and dreary. And to see anew I really have to live in the present; I have to have the present moment be the only thing, the only place where I am at the time."

Thinking keeps us from living in the present moment. Thinking always swings between the past and the future and never alights in the present. I can't *think* of the present, I can only realize or be aware of the present—I can be alive only there. As long as I'm thinking I'm not in the now where I can see and enjoy and live. Realizing this, I've found it helps to simply be aware of what I'm thinking *right now.* When I do, then the thinking which keeps me from the present is now also in the present. So I have nothing distracting to keep me from living in the now.

Tuesday, April 19

Dan was a beautiful man. I was deeply saddened when I heard yesterday that he'd died of cancer. He was gentle and exceptionally spiritually inclined. More than most of us, Dan needed to protect himself against a world of normal people for he lived in an abnormal body.

Dan was crippled severely by arthritis. He needed the support of two canes to get around. He struggled to get into a chair and then struggled to get out. Doing the ordinary things like reaching for a dish in his kitchen cabinet was a chore for him and very painful. He described to me once the extreme physical pain he suffered which no medicine, save strong drugs, could alleviate.

Dan's main problem, though, wasn't physical pain.

5

He'd adapted to that. Dan said that what hurt him most—what caused him excruciating mental pain—was his relationships with women he had loved. Dan never married. Every time he got close to marriage something always happened. He said that almost every time a deep love began to develop his deformed body would get in the way. Usually the women he loved and who claimed to love him would become repulsed by his body. And the relationship would end.

What pain some people suffer. What pain some people go through which we who are "normal" know nothing about. There are so many Dans in the world, so many people right now going through so much misery. I remember when I was in college going around to the veterans' hospitals with our fraternity quartet and trying to entertain the paraplegics, the blind, the injured—all those faces within those wounded bodies, all those faces staring out at you without an expression. It was often impossible to tell whether or not they enjoyed our singing.

After the show came the polite applause, applause coming from people who were understandably so encompassed in their own problems that they couldn't get out of themselves enough to enjoy anything.

All of us suffer pain, it's the nature of the world. But the extreme pain and suffering some people go through seems terribly unfair.

Friday, April 22

Michaelangelo saw this life as a prison formed by matter. All his life he questioned how he could be free of matter and thus free to soar like an eagle, skyward and Godward, into the heavens and beyond. Most of his paintings illustrate this soul-felt desire, this longing to burst the bonds of matter.

For me, feeling the energy of that totally harmonious life is the only experience which can free me from the bonds of matter. To feel that other life, I must let go of my matter-life. Then the life of Spirit becomes evident and is felt.

Saturday, April 23

Descartes said, "I think therefore I am." Rousseau said, in effect, "I feel therefore I am." Both declarations marked giant steps in the understanding and upgrading of the awareness of humanity. Both statements also helped free people from the bonds of authoritarianism perpetrated by the Church and State.

I dream of the day when humanity will take what well may be the final step in the evolutionary spiral of consciousness. This day will come, I believe, when large numbers of people will say, "Because I feel the love which comes from Spirit, *therefore I am.*" Only then, I feel, will we humans be heading on a course away from war, violence and earthly destruction and toward peace and enduring good will among all men.

Monday, April 25

A woman asked me today if the love I was writing about is agape love.* I replied that it isn't.

"Then what kind of love is it?" she asked.

And here I was stuck, for unless one experiences the

---

*John was a columnist for *Vital Signs,* a newsletter for the International Association for Near-Death Studies.

love, feels the love, then there's absolutely no way for words to describe what is meant. It's much like a sighted person attempting to describe to a blind man what the sky is, what the moon is. The blind man would listen to the verbal description and perhaps form a concept about the sky and moon, but he wouldn't know what they actually were like unless he could experience them through sight. Likewise, no amount of verbal describing will ever get another to know what the energy of love is. The energy must be experienced to be known.

Wednesday, April 27

Caroline, Letitia [John's wife] and I* had lunch together at a beautiful little restaurant in town. Just about every week we meet for lunch. It has become a time for asking questions, for searching out the answers, and for discovering anew what a joy there is in discovery. Truly learning with Spirit about life and about Life is a joy indescribable.

Today Letitia brought up the "funnel experience" which we talked about last evening. I first had this experience quite frequently years ago during a time when I was working hard to be with the energy through silencing the mind. As we discussed this, we all began to realize more clearly what causes this kind of experiencing. With the stoppage of the mind, everything which one feels, sees, experiences becomes suspended. Time is gone; there is a loss of consciousness of where or who one is. This, for me, invariably triggers the experience where I feel as if I'm leaving this universe of matter and going through a small aperture, much like a funnel, to emerge again on the other side in a much vaster universe

---

*These three co-authored *Conversations in Spirit*.

of Spirit. Even though I'm not "there" in the ordinary sense of the ego-self being there, a sense of beingness is going on, a sense that my real timeless identity is being revealed—that identity which I feel everyone will experience when going through the physical process called death.

After lunch we parted. I began walking alone toward the library a half dozen blocks away. Recalling what it felt like to emerge into that timeless universe, I just let go. Soon I was there. My body and mind became almost empty of all sensation. And with this inner emptiness, I felt the deep sensing of being. Being was now my life, for there was no interference from self. And I perceived that this beingness felt more outside my body than inside it. Yet it could be detected in both places. It was everywhere.

The flowers along the way looked so incredibly beautiful. The trees were eternal trees. The faces I passed looked radiantly happy, content, harmonious. The buildings, the street, the sky, clouds, cars—all things— were bathed in love and beingness. And they were, because I was seeing from this perfection. Nothing of human judgment was operating. My body was moving I knew not how, but it was keeping pace with being although dead to itself. And with this death was the incredible depth of Spirit's energy. I realized that the mind was especially dead; it was dead through its many layers of consciousness, which was a major reason why the other—Spirit and being—was so strong and full.

All the rest of the day and through most of the evening the body and mind remained stunned and silent. Then during the night when I awoke there was some of this "death" remaining. Consequently, there was some beingness operating even while I slumbered.

This morning it was still with me. While out on my walk it was gentle and loving, vibrant and strong.

This morning while sitting on a rock on an isolated stretch of beach I saw two sandpipers fighting. They would lock their beaks and then, pushing and shoving, they would furiously flap their wings and lunge a few feet into the air before landing back on the ground. This routine kept on until one of them got tired of the fight and flew off.

The victorious bird looked quite proud of itself, that is, until it spotted another sandpiper approaching. It was obvious from the crook in the newcomer's neck and its stalking walk that it was going to challenge the victor. And in a moment they were at it. This time the battle went on for quite a while. They were really going at each other with a fury. Those sharp, long bills were inflicting serious damage. Finally the challenger reared back and stabbed the other bird square in the breast, and came away with a beak full of feathers. This was enough for the hurt bird. With a squawkish yell, it flew off.

Nature, like man, can be mean.

Sunday, May 1

When the reality of Spirit becomes *the* reality for much of humanity then the world will be ready for an illumining by Spirit. At this time I envision Spirit flooding throughout the earth much like the sun floods throughout the land at the dawning of day. Then all materiality will be lifted from the world and the world will be good.

"Do you really think that such an illumining is possible? Visionaries throughout history have fantasized that Utopia was just at hand."

10

I think it's possible but improbable at present, for the materiality of the world will probably continue to keep Spirit's energy from penetrating matter. But who knows? The energy of Spirit is tremendously powerful. So someday it could occur. In the meantime, to live with the energy and to tell others about it and hopefully to have others begin to live with it, is all we can do.

Monday, May 2

Sometimes I just go through a portal and am there. This morning was just such a case. While I was sitting in the patio working in Spirit for others, I just went out of this realm of time, space, and matter and was in the other dimension. It was so simple, so easy. There I was with Spirit, enjoying all the bliss that Spirit enjoys.

And were there other beings there? (Why did this question arise?) I could almost see them, really feel them. Was this imagination, wishful thinking, mental projection? Perhaps. By nature I'm dubious, having seen so much of the imaginative accepted as fact, as truth. This time, though, I could almost feel that whole different world inhabited by spiritual beings, beings who had long ago left this sphere of matter and had gone beyond into the Realm of Love.

Friday, May 6

An acquaintance said that he had died to self to be reborn with Christ. He told me that being identified with Christ gives him a real sense of power to help people.

I feel if one dies to self, in the sense of yielding the body and mind, then it's not necessary to be identified with anything save this sense of loving energy that

11

comes upon one through this death; not only is it not necessary but, I feel, such an identification would be limiting since I would be attempting to approximate my life to Christ's human, temporal life rather than living with the vastness, the infinitude of Spirit's eternal life.

Tuesday, May 10

The "way" one uses to find God doesn't really matter unless we get focused on the way and make that our truth. What does matter is the losing of self. And if this comes through prayer, church, or other means, then so be it; for the life we find when having lost self will teach us, show us how better to be with that Life. Thus there will come a time when the way will drop away, for the experiencing of Spirit and its life will be sufficient.

Saturday, May 14

Day after tomorrow Letitia and I leave for several weeks to camp in California. Am looking forward to it. This form of vacationing, with its closeness to nature has been a delight for both of us and a great aid in deepening with Spirit. There's much joy, freedom and harmony that goes on in our trips.

Sunday, May 15

I walked into the hills above Ojai this Sunday morning and came to a bluff where I could look down upon houses and buildings and thousands of orange trees. The distant murmur of the town just awakening, the chirps and peeps of birds, the soaring of a hawk all formed a beautiful design of sounds and sights which lifted me into a world where all was harmony and peace.

How unsuited I was for the world of business. I was built for this—for mountains and trees and open spaces. I was built for long hours of solitude—hours where I could be alone in nature to watch, listen, be. This, I've discovered, is where insights are given, joys realized, and peace felt. This is where love can flourish—in freedom.

In the past when I was in business how often I needed long times of aloneness. And how seldom I found time to be alone. There was always some demand, some place to be, something in the world that needed to be done.

Mostly it was work that took my time, work and family. The time I spent with my family I loved; I never begrudged this. I did begrudge the amount of time spent at work; it was too much time spent earning a living. By the sweat of our brows we must earn our living, we are told. For me there was too much sweat and not enough solitude.

Nature offers a solace and a peace found nowhere else in the world. In nature I find a freeness, an ability to expand. Here one can more easily leave the pressures and gravitational pulls of the world and enter another realm where love and joy exist. Escapism? Perhaps. And yet perhaps many of us were never meant for the world's activities: its businesses, its conversations, its entertainments, its pleasures, its psychologies and philosophies, its escapes. I find my true being more akin to nature than to the world. I think others feel this way, but many of us never take the steps to adapt our lives to the way we feel, to the way we are. We stay in our spots, in our traps for all too long. I know I did. And I suppose this is understandable for it takes a mighty uprising to free

oneself from the world we have built, built perhaps
before we knew our real selves.

Friday, June 3

Last day of our camping trip. Found lovely, isolated
spots to be and to see.

I never dreamt I could be with a person twenty-four
hours a day, as I have been with Letitia, and be totally
content, totally peace-filled, totally feeling that quality
of solitude even when we're together.

Letitia and I have found that perfect blend of
togetherness and apartness, of conversation and silence,
of sharing and discovering. But I can't in all honesty say
that we have found it. Again, it's Spirit's way of functioning through two people who are similarly inclined.
It's important to be inclined the same way, for if Letitia
required more company, more things, more togetherness
than I, then the lovely, loving balance wouldn't be
there. But she doesn't and the balance is there.

What a God-send Letitia is. Truly God sent her, for I could have never found or figured out that total compatibility factor which we have. Are marriages made in heaven? They almost have to be to work so beautifully.

Wednesday, June 8

So David is gone.* I've shed more tears over his death than all the others.** From a human standpoint, he was about to become a beautiful young man, and then he was crushed. From the standpoint of God, Spirit, Love, David is today what he always was: a being with God.

Sunday, June 12

The pain and suffering, the extreme grief which one feels with the death of a loved one always comes from missing the physicality of the person. Remembrances, images, thoughts all serve to hurt.

The pain must end because when I deepen with the energy I realize that the person—David, me, anyone— doesn't deeply matter. What does matter is the energy of love. This is eternal. This is endless. This is real, the only reality. And if one is fortunate enough or desirous enough to be connected with this love, then one's life is joy no matter what one's problems, no matter what pain one must go through.

---

*John's son, David, age sixteen, was killed on the fourth of June in an auto accident. This was the same day that John and Letitia had returned from their camping trip.

**John's mother, father, brother and sister are all dead.

15

I wrote on David's marker: "A Gentle Being Who Knows Love and is Loved." At first I had written: "A gentle being who knew love and was loved." But my daughter Shanna corrected me and we put the words in the present tense, for I feel that this is the ever-present truth about Dave and all of us.

Beautiful David did matter to us. And the stupidity of his death—its non-sense-less-ness—is hard sometimes to bear.

It's hard sometimes not to feel anger toward the boy responsible for Dave's death. [It was determined that the boy driving the car which David was in was negligent.] And yet I realize anger is such a harmful emotion and so far from the energy of love that I feel. Also I realize that anger or any hard emotion can keep one from melting into the energy. So when I do get to thinking about the accident and anger arises, I remember these things and quickly drop the thoughts and turn again to Spirit.

So Dave is no longer here. Someday all of us will be no longer here. How do we conduct our lives in view of this fact, in view of this truth?

I find it helpful in the handling of Dave's death to get down to the hard facts and deal with them. The hard facts are that Dave is gone and that's that. It does no one any good to keep ruminating on the feelings of separation, on the feelings of never seeing him again. To be able to look at one's memories, to look at the many times we were together—mostly happy, love-filled times—and not feel the pain of grief, this is a tremendous overcoming and a by-product, I know, of feeling the energy.

Tuesday, June 22

The other morning I went down by the ocean and sat on a rock. The hurt of missing David was immense. Spirit was with me, but the memories and the hurt seemed stronger than Spirit. And I began to consider these times of grief. After awhile I asked: What is it that's suffering? How does suffering arise? Though I had asked myself this same question dozens of times before, I was looking for a fresh insight, a renewed perspective, a current truth to work with.

The answer which came was the same answer which had come many times before: It's this *me* that's suffering. That's the only thing that can suffer.

As I considered this insight the process of suffering slowly became unveiled. I began to see that a thought, a memory, an image of David would come to mind— perhaps the image of the last time we talked, or the last time we played tennis, or the last time we hugged. And I would realize that these things would never be again. With this realization would come the tears and with the tears the deep gnawing pain of grief. And I saw that unless this cycle stopped then the grief could go on forever.

So I asked myself: What will stop this cycle; what will stop the endless round of thoughts and images which are causing me such grief? And I saw that it was me

17

separating myself from the feeling of grief which caused much of grief's continuance. I perceived that the remedy for this rift, the remedy for this separation between me and the grief I was experiencing was to get as close to the feeling of grief as possible.

So I began to look within directly at the grief. I began to get the feeling of grief in sharp focus. I felt grief's pain, its anguish, it's unmitigated horror. I felt its emptiness, its barrenness, its desperateness. I felt all those feelings that we try all our lives to avoid. At first the hurt was excruciating and made me want to turn away, to escape, to avoid. But I knew that was no good. I knew I must stick with it, for to try to escape would keep the pain going.

So I stayed with the feelings of grief. And as I did I felt the gap between myself and my pain, between myself and my feelings of grief, slowly close. Now I felt less of me, thus I felt less pain. But I knew it was important to keep on, for there were other changes taking place. Now I was feeling a tremendous inner intensity. It was as if a laser beam was focused at the back of my head and was boring right through all my feelings, through all my thoughts.

The process continued. The process deepened. There was now no longer a me, no longer an I. And without this me there was no more suffering. But there was something else happening. There was a realm of life, of love, of infinitude which was within, without, all around me. Yet it wasn't me who was experiencing this life for the me wasn't there. The life of love was there. An intensity of awareness was there. And within the intensity there was an awareness of this life of love. Was the intensity part of this love? It seemed that way. But it was important during this timeless time not to question, not to verbalize, not to be drawn into the me with its thinkings and questionings.

So while I was sitting on that rock that day by the ocean, a deeper healing for grief began. It was the healing energy of love, the intensity of awareness and getting lost to self, which was bringing it about.

I see again that the pain one suffers is always ego-pain—the pain suffered by this bundle of pent-up energy we call ourselves. If we can find some way to die to this me, to get rid of this self, then the pain of suffering ends; it must, for there's no longer an entity left to suffer.

This is the reason I believe that drugs are used so profusely when one is going through hard times, through times of sorrow, for drugs afford a form of death, a form of numbing oneself to pain and suffering. But the problem with using drugs is that the relief is always temporary and can lead into other problems. So I see once again how important it is to find a natural way to lose self, a natural way to have the me discontinue.

What is this me that we think is our life? It's just a bunch of thoughts, memories, experiences wrapped up in a Self-Package, through which we experience daily life.

Unless I can find ways, naturally, of unwrapping the Self-Package then I'm destined to meet daily life with the old contents of self, which is to miss experiencing life anew.

Thursday, June 24

This morning while watching the seagulls soaring in the wind, I got lost. It was such a beautiful release from the recent heavy emotions I've felt. And I noticed that in my "lostness"—behind, above, below, beyond—there was an incredible infinitude of space, of love, of beauty, of joy, anything that might describe absolute freedom and perfection. It wasn't so much that I was sensing the freedom and perfection. It was that I was feeling it through a sense beyond the human senses: I was in a different sphere where grief, self-consciousness, effort, conflict—everything disharmonious—was gone.

After a while I became aware that the leaves, the flowers, the grass—everything about me—were filled with light and a lightness. Nature had lost some of its opaqueness; matter was less dense, at least this is how it appeared to the eyes which were transformed and perceiving. It was an incredible journey into eternity and joy, one from which I wanted never to return.

Monday, July 4

This morning after I'd climbed over the barbed wire fence and had begun my walk along the cliffs next to the ocean, I felt that beautiful internal release of all the energy within my body. It felt as if a faucet had been turned on and all the body's energy began to drain away. And with the draining of the body's energy, I began to feel an increase of the harmonious energy.

What an incredible joy it is, what an incredible gift it is to feel the energy. By feeling it, I was truly a new person. I had a new identity. Before feeling the depths of the energy, I had unconsciously identified myself humanly. Now I realized that I was part of the energy I was feeling. Before feeling Spirit's energy deeply, I was operating to a large degree from the human energy system. Now through feeling the new energy, I was moving, living, being, communing from another energy system, a system far removed from and diametrically opposed to the physical one.

I was especially grateful for this depth of Spirit today,

for the memories of Dave were quite severe and painful. To feel the energy is not an escape from the pain, for with it you can remember all the joyous times you had with the person and not have it hurt. You can look at the fact that you won't be seeing him again here on earth and even that doesn't hurt.

Sunday, July 10

When he heard about David's death, a friend from back east sent me a book about the overcoming of grief. The author's premise—she also had had a child die—was that we need to go through the "process". By this she meant we need to open ourselves up to memories that hurt, to feelings that hurt, to thoughts that hurt; never should we try to escape from the hurt, for by escaping we're suppressing and therefore will someday pay the consequences.

For me, going through the process isn't so helpful, for it creates a duality which is the basis of the ego and thus the continuance of pain. To view grief from a distance as me and my grief, as me and my thoughts and as me and my painful memories can never really deeply help to overcome grief for me. What can help and did help immensely was to commune with life—with people, thoughts, feelings, memories, the birds, animals— everything. Through communing—which is drawing ever so close to things so that you're really a part of all life—the pain is bound to go, for the self is gone. Then the energy, to some degree, is there. And the energy is always healing, is always overcoming everything that is material, and grief is certainly one of the most material feelings in life.

So when painful memories of Dave arise, which inevitably they do, then I draw close to the memories and

the pain. I also draw close to everything at hand. As the
gap closes between myself and the memories, between
myself and everything else, the pain of separation
naturally goes. And what is there in pain's place is the
energy of love.

Tuesday, July 19

This morning on my walk I was feeling weak and
quite disabled from a physical problem. Realizing now
was the time to get radical and really go after the sensations, I let go of the body. Feeling the energy increase, I
yielded still further which allowed the energy to grow
and deepen. Then I *went into* the energy.

Such total immersion into the energy is a healing
balm. This morning I was so totally immersed that all
bodily sensations disappeared. After a while I began
quite naturally to realize more deeply who I really am;

22

and who I am, I saw, is the energy of Spirit I was feeling at that very moment. Who I am is the pure, untouched energy which I was totally immersed in right then. Thus I could state silently and with honesty that the energy I was feeling was the strength of my being, for I could feel the truth of these words. I could silently state that the energy was my health, for I could feel the truth of this. I could silently state that the energy was the perfection of my being, for as I was immersed in that purity there was no imperfection to be found anywhere. Therefore the present imperfection manifesting in my body was not the truth of Spirit or the truth of me, who was at this time a part of Spirit. Thus the imperfection was entirely without reality.

What a release. What a relief. I was in a different realm where all is perfection and pure, where all is totally untouched by anything of this world—by any physical energy, the energy of matter, which is such a blight on the world.

When the depth of the immersion diminished and I was back again feeling more of this physical realm, I realized that the physical weakness and the other symptoms were almost gone.

Thursday, July 21

The minister was head of the largest church of its kind. He had once been president of the church's national organization, so he was well versed in the church's beliefs and doctrines.

When I was a small boy my parents insisted that I attend this church. Obediently, I went along, but as I got older I began to see that the minister's ideas and beliefs weren't mine; his feelings about life weren't my feelings; nor were his or the Bible's perceptions of Jesus as being

23

the Savior of the world something I could accept. I felt then as I do today that Jesus was a man filled with God's Spirit, God's life, but this didn't make him the Savior. What it did make him, in my estimation, was a forerunner showing us what we can potentially be—a person filled with the energy and life of Spirit.

So when I entered a college about a hundred miles from home I was finally free not to go to church. And I didn't. Still, I wasn't free of the minister's fervor, for every time he'd see me, (John occasionally sang at the church when he was home on weekends) he would try in various ways to get me back into the fold. He was sincere and dedicated in his efforts, but they sometimes were a little too much.

Even after six years of college, a year or so of being married, and less and less contact with the minister, I still hadn't been forgotten. One day he dropped by the house. This time he not only focused on me, but he was also determined to save my wife who was the daughter of a minister of a more liberal denomination.

I remember that he sat in the chair next to the front window trying to convince us that if we just accepted Jesus we could be assured of eternal life and of being together in heaven after we died.

Finally, I said that no one could be sure of that since no one knows what happens after death. Maybe, I said, it's what Socrates said about death: It's an endless sleep.

Well, such talk didn't set well with the minister, and soon he left. I didn't talk to him again for about twenty years. Then, while I was visiting my parents in Florida, a call came in from him. He said that his wife of fifty-five years had just recently died. When he found out I was visiting he asked to speak to me. As we talked, he said that over the years he'd often reflected on our conversations, and though he still disagreed with me, he could better see my position in view of his recent tragedy. He said that he never thought God would let him end up this way—alone and in ill health. He really felt that God would have taken better care of both him and his wife because of their life-long dedication to doing God's work, but it just hadn't worked out that way. Now all he had to look forward to was joining his wife in Heaven.

Then he said, "You know, John, maybe none of us knows for sure what this life is all about."

Wednesday, August 3

A beautiful practitioner of healing said to me recently that all of her healings were effected by simply affirming the "truth." She said she has had many healings of all kinds of diseases through using only mental affirmations. She maintains that if these affirmations aren't true then they wouldn't work.

When I feel the energy and become immersed in the energy then there's a natural affirmation, or, I'd rather put it that there's a natural realization of who I am and what my relationship to the energy is. Then I can state honestly that my being is with Spirit and know the truth of this statement because I'm feeling that kinship right at the moment.

One should be cautious about using affirmations too frequently, I feel, for they could end up becoming one's truth rather than the love we feel from Spirit being one's truth.

A dear lady once told me that all her life she'd been affirming "truth" and yet she'd had very little results. Then she related a heart-rending story about her husband who had contracted cancer. All through this terrible episode she would endlessly sit by his bedside affirm-

25

ing and repeating to him the truth of his being. And at her insistence, he would repeat these same affirmations.

"And yet it didn't work," she said sorrowfully. "He died a long and painfully slow death."

Sunday, August 7

This material world is bound by time and space; the world of Spirit is eternal and infinite. This world's substance is matter; the substance of Spirit's world is its essence, which is Spirit. This world is plagued by sickness, accidents and death; Spirit's world is absolute wholeness, harmony, and eternal life.

Living in this material world, we attempt to make sense of it; we attempt to make it into something which it's not—God's creation—for surely God who is love, truth, harmony, absolute goodness and perfection couldn't have created a world so different from himself.

When I take a material feeling—a feeling of discomfort, for instance—and try to find the source of that feeling by following it back, I find that I enter a world somewhat like Spirit's: a world of freedom and matter-sensationless being.

What's happening here? Could it be that matter originally emanated from Spirit? If so, somewhere along the way there was a disconnect—matter burst away, for some reason, from Spirit.

Whatever the cause, if indeed such a premise is correct, the fact is that matter-feelings are not at all like the feelings generated by the energy of Spirit. They are definitely dissimilar. The evil inherent in matter-feelings occur when these feelings get focused, get intensified; then they manifest as pain, sickness, physical death.

Thursday, August 11

Martin Heidegger (the existential philosopher) said that a major cause of disharmony between people and nations can be found in the perception that we are the subject—the entity who is of primary importance in life—and everyone else is an object. He maintains that this subject/object relationship is man's rationale for dominating other people, for going to war, for murdering, for stealing, for perpetrating all manners of evil against one's fellow man.

Martin Buber (German-Israeli philosopher) similarly saw that as long as people feel alienated from each other major difficulties must exist in relationships between individuals and nations. Thus he concluded that we should conceive of ourselves in an I/thou relationship where one perceives our I in the thou—the other person. This, he felt, would serve to end the alienation process and inaugurate empathy, understanding and true compassion between people.

Krishnamurti has likewise seen that the self's separation from its thoughts, experiences, things and other people is the basis of all conflict within man and within man's relationships. He maintains that to actually experience the truth that the thinker is the thought, that the person is his experience, is the highest form of power and realization. And, he maintains, the experiencing of this fusion will produce a transformation, a mutation at the deepest levels of the mind.

This morning I was considering this question of feeling divided and separated from people, from things and from one's inner thoughts and feelings. At the time I was feeling a great deal of the energy, and as I looked within I saw that all division between myself and anything else was gone. It wasn't that I didn't recognize a body that is separate and different from all else around me, but that was incidental because the energy I was feeling is a life, an existence, a love whose very nature is union and wholeness.

So as I was deeply feeling that unbroken and unifying energy and experiencing my relationship to that energy, all my feelings of separateness were naturally gone— without any effort on my part. They were non-existent. There was only a feeling of union, harmony and communion with all that was about.

Friday, August 12

I really think, if we're truly seeking for the Ultimate and honestly acknowledge that we don't know what that Ultimate is, then Spirit brings us those persons, books, ideas—the Teachers—who can help us. It's an individual thing because each one of us is in a different place and needs different temporary solutions. The important thing, I think, is not to get stuck with the Teachers. Rather we should keep moving toward that one and only Reality—Spirit Itself. And when that's found then the Teachers who have helped along the way become much less important, even though one always will be grateful to them and for them.

Woke up this morning with a sensation of fever. As I worked with the energy against the sensation, I began to realize that I needed to get beyond the *recognition* of this feeling. This was often extremely helpful in dealing with the cancer.* To get beyond the recognition of the feeling, I saw it was necessary to strip the *word* fever away from the feeling. The reason this is important is that the word keeps the feeling going.

But I found it very difficult to strip the word away from the feeling of fever, for my mind has always dealt with its feelings on a verbal level. To try to break that habit, that conditioning, required persistence; it required a stick-to-itiveness no matter how long it took. And this was the challenge: To persevere despite feeling a lack of energy and drive to do so.

So as I sat in my chair by the window, every time my mind would refer to the word *fever*, I'd strip the word away. Finally, I felt the word *fever* starting to lose its importance, to lose its connotations and lose its attachments to the thing it was describing. And with the impact of the word slowly departing, I found myself, somewhat later, at a place beyond the word. Now I was left with the nakedness of the pure feeling.

So what do I do now? I continued to stick with the feeling. I didn't let it go. I continued not to verbalize the feeling. After a while I found myself at that place of not

---

*John had cancer in 1974.

recognizing the feeling I once called fever, for I had gone beyond the recognition of the feeling.

Now the feeling started to go, it started to dissolve. I realized it was going because its total support system had been destroyed. Whereas before the feeling was kept alive by the word *fever* and by my recognition of the feeling which that word represented, now these were both gone. Thus I was beyond the feeling of fever. The fever was totally gone! And not only this, but I found myself in a totally different dimension of life, a dimension where all was freedom, joy, harmony.

This same process, I feel, can be applied to any and all negative feelings whether we call them loneliness, grief, pain, jealousy, fear, cancer, anything, for all feelings are generated or received by the human mind. Thus when the human mind is transcended, gone beyond, then the feelings which it experiences must cease.

I hope that someday the medical profession will experiment with this process to find out if it could help cancer patients and other suffering people. The question is: Can others do this? It might take some time, it might take some training, but I know it's possible, especially when the person awakens to the fact that the mind can produce feelings of cancer. In fact, the mind—the lower, more dense, material aspect of the mind which we call the body—*is* these feelings.

"How could the mind be a major cause of cancer?"

We see how the mind affects the body. So why couldn't the mind, with its fearful conscious and unconscious thoughts about cancer, burn these thoughts upon the body?

"But present medical knowledge says that viruses cause cancer."

I'm sure viruses attend cancer. But are they the cause or affect? Certainly if we inject cancer cells into living organisms then often cancer results. But is this a physical process or a mental one? And are the physical and mental processes one in the same?

"Certain products, such as carcinogens in cigarettes, cause cancer. That's been proved."

Then why don't all heavy smokers—persons who have puffed cigarettes for fifty or sixty years—get it?

"Someday man will develop a vaccine against cancer. This will prove that the mind is not the culprit."

I deeply hope that we will develop a vaccine. But I don't think this will prove that the mind isn't a major cause of cancer. What it will reveal once again, I believe, is that there's intercommunication between the mind/body. Thus, when the mind/body accepts the "fact" that the vaccine will immunize, then cancer will be no more.

The mind *is* the body and the body is part of the mind. What affects one, affects the other.

Sunday, August 14

A woman wrote me the other day to ask how we heal with the energy, for she knew from our books that we'd had many healings. When I was asked this same question many years ago, I replied that the first thing I do is to get John Allan out of the way, for I can't do anything to heal another person. Spirit—the energy—is the healer. Therefore I must get out of the way to allow the energy to flow through me, for only then can I direct this healing energy toward a person.

So what is directing? How does one direct the energy? I've usually responded that people will find a way to direct the energy of love they feel in a way they intuit or are shown. The point is first to feel the energy through a deep yielding of the body. Then if one deeply wants to help another person, the way to direct—get the energy to that person—will be found.

I direct in the way I was shown that day in Santa Barbara when I "knew" I was going to die from the cancer. At the very instant that I said to God, "I'm going to die unless you help me," I felt a tremendous release inside— all the struggling to save my life ended. With this there came an incredible inpouring of the energy. It felt as if everything inside the body had been cleansed away, emptied, and all that was left in the empty shell was the energy.

So when I am directing, the first thing I do is to release the body—empty it out—so that the energy can channel through. Then it's simply a matter of sending the energy to the other person.

Directing to one's self can help one immensely to deepen with the energy. It can also heal the body, as has been proved time and again. When directing to myself I simply release the body and allow the energy to go to the places where I feel material energy—that is, the human senses.

When directing to myself I often feel a melting of the bodily senses, and this naturally makes the energy more full. At these times, I realize the real substantialness of the energy. It feels, at times, more substantial than the physical body and thus more real than the body. I've referred to this substantialness as a Pillar of Power. It feels as though there's a pillar running from the Source of the energy, Spirit, right through my body. The inner substance of the pillar is an incredibly pure, untouched energy which is empty of everything worldly but filled with a massive amount of energy.

I'm reminded of how directing was first given. I had just returned from Santa Barbara. As I was walking to the post office to pick up my mail, several friends and acquaintances inside a small restaurant motioned for me to join them. As we sat talking, I noticed a neighbor of mine, sitting across the table, staring intently at me.

After we left the restaurant she took me aside and asked, "What were you doing in there?" Then she explained that she had felt the most marvelous sense come over her. "It was joy, that's the only way to describe it."

I told her I wasn't doing anything. I was, however, feeling a great deal of the energy and evidently she was picking it up.

Later, as I thought about it, I began to wonder if others might be able to pick up the energy. So I began to experiment with directing the energy toward my children when they were sick. I found that they recovered much faster than they had in the past. Many times their healings were immediate. Shanna's asthma was healed instantly. And Linda's (John's older daughter) eye problem, which the doctors said was incurable without an operation, was healed in just a few days.

There were others who contacted me for healings. For the most part the results were quite remarkable. And with almost every healing the people felt the energy. That was the beautiful thing, for this made them realize that there is another sense of life "out there" which is joyous and loving and can heal their bodies.

To heal someone it's important to listen to the person who is sick. Through listening, we can discover the blockages that need to be removed so that the energy of Spirit will have free access into the person.

I listened to a man on the telephone last night. He had called from Georgia and was asking us for help because his health was failing. As we talked I found out that the cancer he had five years ago was again active. Also diabetes was a problem which was causing his eyes to weaken.

All the while we talked I listened carefully to find out

if he had one central concern. Finally it came out that he was terrified of dying a long, slow, and painful death. Now I knew the major blockage was fear, as it usually is. This gave me a direction in which to move. We now must work diligently with Spirit to remove the fear. And with its removal, the body I'm sure will respond positively.

Sunday, August 21

Two members of a local church knocked at my door this morning. They were polite and got to the point quickly saying they were there to talk to me about God, prophecy and what their religion said about both.

I listened for a while and then asked why they believed that their beliefs were the true beliefs. If they'd been raised a Buddhist or Moslem, would they be espousing these beliefs? They answered yes; for in some way, through some "voice" or intuition, they would have learned of the truth of God and the Bible no matter where they'd been born or what upbringing they had.

I then asked why they accepted the founder of their religion's teachings over someone else's. Their response was that their founder took his teachings directly from the Bible which was the word of God.

Finally I queried them about why they didn't think they could experience Truth or God directly for themselves. Then they wouldn't have to rely on creeds and beliefs and doctrines. They responded that they often went directly to God in prayer. But that wasn't enough. They needed to know what God had in store for them, what He wanted them to do, how He wanted them to act. These things the founder of their religion taught them.

After they'd gone, I wondered why I had spent so

much time with them and they with me. Neither I nor they were going to change the other's mind, though each of us might have hoped to. For myself, I hoped that they would take a broader look at this whole issue of religion, God, and life; for their part, they felt they had the answer to religion, God, and life, and it was now imperative that they share these answers with persons like me hopefully to convert my mind and heart.

Thursday, August 25

Been reading more of Simone Weil.* She really seems like an intelligent woman, one who's dedicated to the spiritual life and teaching this life to others. In the article I just read, she stresses the point that learning should develop the power of attention, which not only lightens the mind but also allows one to make contact with God or Reality! Quite a statement. Quite a challenge.

Krishnamurti also emphasizes the value of attention. He contends that through a high state of attention, which is the outcome of observing "what is," the ego disappears. I think he's right, for as I've experimented over the years with attending intently to an object or internal feeling, I've found that in such attention almost all thought is burned away. And without thought there is no ego, for the ego requires thought to keep itself alive—the ego has been manufactured by thought. Now without thought there comes an incredible clarity, a translucent way of seeing and understanding. Whereas before the mind was struggling to see and understand, now through attention the process is effortless.

I've also found that to attend deeply to anything for too long can produce a "pulling one's self up by one's

*French essayist and educator.

bootstraps" feeling which can defeat the purpose of attention.

Attention for me is the nonmovement of thought. With thought's movement ended, there's the discerning of another movement—that of the immensity of Creation itself. Now one is in contact with that timeless movement, that timeless life. One is part of it, not the one who is a particular consciousness—the individual—but that part of us which is universal.

Saturday, August 27

Went for a walk on the beach this morning. The sky was gray and the ocean was the same. Even the sea gulls seemed lifeless, listless, content to sit together on the sand and doze away the morning hours.

On days like these I've sometimes found it more difficult to feel Spirit deeply, but today for some reason I felt that incredible sense of joy inside. And as I "went into it" I realized that I felt empty inside—all the things of self just weren't there. There was only joy, peace, contentedness. And I asked myself: Were these feelings there because of the emptiness, or were they there because joy, peace, contentedness are the qualities of that emptiness—are the very nature of that emptiness which really is a fullness? I think it's the latter.

Sunday, August 28

Just been reading some Swedenborg* this evening. How objective he is oftentimes in his scientific analysis of secular things. But when he comes to the matter of Faith and Doctrine, he becomes quite subjective, I feel.

His belief about the correspondence between this world of matter and the world of spirit needs to be questioned, I think, for to propose that this world has ultimate meaning because it is a preparation for our future spirit-life doesn't always seem to meet the facts. Right now I'm thinking about all those people who die early. How much preparation and learning did they have? Was David's life a preparation for spirit-life? Certainly he felt more Spirit than most people, but I hardly think that at sixteen this world had prepared him for the next world. I wonder if it ever does, for how can matter existence prepare us for spirit-existence? The two are diametrically opposite.

Just the other evening I read about the murder of an outstanding student and athlete. He was about to embark on studies at Princeton with every potential to bring the world something beautiful and beneficial. But he was brutally murdered for no apparent motive at all.

Also I think of the hundreds, perhaps thousands of people in the world right today, who have met similar fates. How many people in the past have had their lives

---

*Swedish scientist and theologian.

cut short before they were able to fulfill their potentials? How many people in the future will have similar fates befall them? This is the way life is for so many people.

Monday, August 29

A theory, a speculation really, which came to me this morning is that all life—both the life we call Spirit and the life we call matter—originated from one Energy Source. But how could this be; how could a life which is perfect—Spirit—and a life which is imperfect—matter— emanate from a common source? And I saw, surmised, that perhaps what we call matter-life simply doesn't recognize that it has come from the energy of Spirit. Consequently matter-life assumes that it has been born into a life of isolation, of exile, of alienation, of self-conscious struggle.

But such assumptions aren't true (or so the theory goes) if, in fact, all life derives from God, Spirit, for matter-existence is just as directly connected to and par-ticipating with Spirit as spirit-existence. Thus matter-existence itself couldn't be suffering feelings of isolation and struggle. So how did we get into this fix? How did we get into into this enigmatic, problematic, and paradoxical world of matter?

Could it be that somewhere along the way—right as we were cradled in the womb of Spirit, right as we were perfectly taken care of by Love and living in an endless state of bliss—that a self-conscious thought arose which wondered aloud what it would be like to experience a life separate from Spirit? And from that thought might there not have occurred a terrible rending? And as the rending grew might it not have brought about a great explosion—the Big Bang—which inaugurated the world of matter?

Certainly all this is mere conjecture and unverifiable. What is verifiable is that a life separate from Spirit must be a life opposite to Spirit, and matter-life is just such a life. For in the world of matter we experience every imperfection and disharmony imaginable, which is just the opposite to Spirit's life of perfection and absolute harmony.

But the fact is (in theory of course) that we don't *actually* live in a world of matter; we don't *actually* live in a world separate from Spirit. We think we do, but in fact we don't. And this is verifiable, for when we are quiet enough, at peace enough, harmonious enough, we can feel our life still cradled in the womb of Spirit.

Thursday, September 1

After a beautiful, transcendent day and evening yesterday, I experienced, last night, a continuous series of conflictive dreams. I remember Aldous Huxley once said, when he experienced similar disturbances after practicing Zen meditations, that he felt such disturbances come from the mind trying to reclaim itself; it was trying to reclaim itself because it felt threatened that these experiences might remove it from its time-and-material-based way of experiencing the world.

Perhaps Huxley is right; perhaps the mind does feel threatened by such experiences and feels the need to strike back, to get itself again on a mechanical, sensate basis. But I wonder if there might not be another analysis of the situation. I wonder if these disturbances might not be attributed to a negative force or energy of this material world.

If Spirit's world is real—and it is real for me and others who feel it—then this world of matter must be cloaked in unreality, for Spirit's world and matter's world can't both be real—real in the sense of being absolute, eternal, perfect. Thus what is unreal might have—likely will have—many unrealities, the greatest of which, perhaps, is a negative energy or evil sense of life which is opposite to and opposing the sense of goodness, beauty and love which is the essence of Spirit's life.

Huxley once speculated that the waters at Lourdes heal because of the tens of thousands of people who poured upon the shrine their good and loving thoughts and feelings. This, he said, perhaps created a force for good which heals the body. If his theory is correct, then why couldn't the opposite be true? Why couldn't the tens of thousands of negative, horror-filled, hate-filled, revenge-filled thoughts which are poured daily upon the world create an evil power? If in fact this is true, then Jesus' statement about evil being a self-created entity (in John 8:44 Jesus states that evil has created itself) is comprehensible, for if negative thoughts and feelings have created an entity of evil, then such an entity has fathered itself and is thus lacking an actual source, a *raison d'etre* which makes it in effect a myth, an unreality.

Sunday, September 4

This morning while sitting on a rock on an isolated stretch of beach, I considered how thought and images keep one imprisoned in the world. Everything around me spoke of an image, which in turn became a thought, which in turn created a sensation, which in turn fueled more thought and images. Seeing the inner dilemma, I just let go of my body and mind, my life. Immediately I began to feel that inner space where all is filled with joy. And as I looked within I saw not an image, I saw not a

thought or a human sensation. There, all was peace.
There, my true being was—my being with Spirit.

Monday, September 5

I met a direct person today, one who looked me
square in the eyes, without any defenses or pretenses,
and expressed something real which she was thinking
and feeling. She is a neighbor and she was riding her
bike around getting some air and exercise.

For a few minutes we shared, we communicated, we
communed. What we talked about was less important
than what we were feeling.

As we parted she said, "I always enjoy talking to
you."

"And I, you," I stated.

How beautiful it was that for a brief moment two
people had met.

Tuesday, September 6

A woman said to me recently that she knew her
religion is the truth because it had worked so many
times for her. It had worked to heal her; it had worked
in finding her a mate; it had worked in providing her
family with more money; it had worked to establish harmony in her life. It had done all these things and so
much more.

I thought to myself: There are so many things that
work in life. Positive thinking works. Affirming works.
Astrology works. Biofeedback works. Medicine works.
Faith works. Hard work works. But just because

something works, does this make it truth? Or is truth of a dimension entirely different from this world, a dimension of pure and eternal love where the question of what works or what doesn't work never arises.

Wednesday, September 7

The energy of love *is* harmony; there is no disharmony or conflict therein. To be in contact with this energy is to live a life filled with harmony, joy and oftentimes bliss. This energy is there for everyone's participation. To have this energy within us, we must discover ways to yield the energy of friction—the body/mind energy—for this energy which animates the human being leaves no room for us to feel love's harmonious energy. With the yielding of friction's energy, the energy of love is there.

Many of our relationship problems center on the division between people created by our self-conscious concerns. When I'm concerned only about my security, my bank account, my family, my problems, and the other person is concerned only about his, then these concerns inhibit us from ever deeply relating and caring about each other. If we don't deeply care about each other, this leads to a sense of callousness. Such callousness and noncaring then ripple out from our microcosmic life into the macrocosm of the world.

Desire distorts. One can even feel Spirit deeply and desire can supersede. I can have the most altruistic motives and still find my desire getting in the way of Spirit. In fact, the more altruistic my desire, the easier it is for me to focus on that first and Spirit second. Not purposely, it just happens.

Desire is unclarity. If I desire something strongly then confusion clouds my vision; I don't see the simple facts. Not that I refuse to, I just don't, for I can't. Desire creates justification, rationalization, self-will, all of which lead away from Spirit.

So what can we do if we have a strong desire for something, if we just can't remain passive in the face of what we want? I think then it takes a cooling down, a standing back for a while and looking at things. For if I go plunging in following the leadings of my desire, then I'm lost and probably will cause hurt and harm to myself and to others. But if I can take a long, hard look at my desire and then turn desire's feelings over to the energy of Spirit, desire is naturally and easily tempered —the fire of desire naturally calms and gradually dims.

Now we have a situation where the desire of the mind and the senses has been replaced with the energy of Spirit. Now there is no distortion. Now there is simple clarity. Now desire is no longer in command—Spirit is. So now we can look from Spirit's vantage point and take an overview of the whole problem of desire and see it from a wholeness, see it from perfection. Then we'll know if we're in accord with Spirit's wholeness and perfection. If we are, we'll proceed knowing that we'll not be hurting or harming anyone, but rather bringing a blessing to all.

Thursday, September 8

A friend and I had been discussing the difference between self-consciousness and being conscious of Spirit. And what a difference there is. Within self-consciousness are all the confines of matter. Self-consciousness *is* material consciousness—it's our sole connection with matter. Within self-consciousness are all our feelings of matter, which produce all our material thoughts. Self-consciousness creates our awareness and belief in matter—it creates our imprisonment in matter, thus our unhappiness. It's the central cause of our unhappiness. Being conscious of Spirit, on the other hand, creates an opposite sensing of life, an opposite experiencing—a joyous one.

"I agree," said my friend. "Self-consciousness is a prison and does cause our unhappiness. But how do we get out of the prison?"

It seems to me that we need to drop self-conscious-ness. I think it's as simple and as difficult as this. It's simple because the dropping of self is a motiveless act—it just happens through an awareness that it's necessary if we're to experience freedom in life. It's difficult because there's so much of the world in each one of us—a steady programming going on inside. This pro-gram needs to be disconnected, to be done with, which is not at all easy. But it is simple.

If we disconnect the program, which is our individual tap-in to the world, then there naturally comes an ele-ment of the energy. In the energy is total freedom, for the energy is totally unself-conscious. And as we par-ticipate with it, we become more unself-conscious, which brings freedom from the prison of matter.

While walking on a bluff that overlooks the ocean, I deeply let go of the body's life and felt the energy of Spirit building, growing and then flowing outward beyond all limitation. Truly the energy is infinite. With it there are no boundaries.

As I looked up the beach, I saw a house with pink flowers luminating the front lawn. I looked up to the hilltop and saw the trees and shrubs standing out starkly against the morning sky. My eyes wandered to the ocean

where I watched the pelicans gliding silently across the gray sea.

The marvel was that everything my eyes perceived, I was with. I was actually there with these things because I had left the here—the limitation of the body. Because of Spirit and its infinite energy, I had broken through matter and was reaching out and touching all.

Friday, September 9

A hawk had a mouse clutched tightly in its talons. He lit on the top of a light pole and peered down at me. The little mouse was struggling to get free, but it was useless to fight against those ruthless claws. The hawk began to rip the mouse apart and eat it. I heard the mouse squeak. It squirmed. It squealed. The hawk continued to rip and eat. The hawk had no compassion for the mouse. It was conditioned not to.

On this earth there's death everywhere, not only with the birds, animals and man but with everything that lives. The flowers wither and die. The trees get old and diseased and slowly die. The grasses of the field live a short while and then become shriveled in death to be restored in the spring with the gentle rains. Everything on the earth is vulnerable to death. And one asks why.

The familiar answers are that creation and destruction are complementary processes which eventually lead to good. Or, because original man sinned and fell from Grace, God is now punishing the descendents of this first man by allowing death, disease and destruction to be. Another answer is that through the death of one form of life—the mouse—another life—the hawk—lives. Of all the answers, this last one seems the most cruel.

If I don't accept these answers because they don't meet the facts of Spirit's life, then what can I think about death, disaster, and destruction, which are everywhere? Before I can answer this I find I must enter Spirit's dimension where none of these deathly dark qualities of life exist, for it's only from there that I can look back at this world and see it objectively— see it clearly for what it is.

When I have made the transition to Spirit's realm and then look back at this world, I see that the world of matter is a waking sense-dream much like our sleeping sense-dreams. I also see that this dream where death and evil are dominant emanates from and maintains itself through material sensations, which create in our dream a material consciousness. Without these sensations this world would not be for us, for we would have lost all consciousness of the world. These material sensations constitute the material world and every living thing within it. These sensations are the sense of life for every organism, every animal, and perhaps for every flower and tree.

I also see that it's through and because of material sensation that every person and every living creature emerges into the world. When material man and creature lose these sensations, then they are perceived to be unconscious or dead. All physical life and death are based on these sensations. These sensations constitute the Hypothetical Man—the material entity who lives a short time entrapped in matter before dying out of matter.

Looking from Spirit's dimension, I perceive this Hypothetical Man for what he is—a material imitation of our real identity with Spirit. Thus I see how important it is that this Man yields his material sensations for they are perceived as his life. And when the Man comes to this point of realization and acts upon it, then he naturally begins to feel the life of Spirit.

Now when the Hypothetical Man begins sensing Spirit's life, he finds that much of his self-conscious, material dream-life begins to fade away, for he has lost much material sensing of himself. And as he moves deeper into that life of Spirit, he sees that there is a another Man or identity standing right in the place where he was awhile ago. This other Man is not a part of matter but a part of Spirit's life, a part of Spirit's joy and perfection, a part of Spirit's deathless eternity. Unlike the Hypothetical Man, he sees that there's no longer any waiting for physical death to usher him into that other realm. Being part of Spirit, this Man sees that he's participating with eternal life right here and now.

Sunday, September 11

Someone asked me why I was so devoted to this life of Spirit. They said that they could never be since the world is so captivating.

The world can be captivating. For years, before I

learned that Spirit is real and got it identified as something I could experience daily, I lived a fairly worldly life. Then after feeling Spirit for a while, my whole outlook changed. I began to look at life in the world's sense as much less of a life than the life of Spirit.

So as I increasingly experienced the energy of Spirit's eternal life, it gradually dawned on me that there is no other real life to be devoted to. The world's life became of little concern to me, save for the helping of others and the sharing of Spirit's life.

Thursday, September 15

Walked to a remote section of beach last evening to watch the sunset. It was unusual not to see anyone, even in this out-of-the-way spot. For a timeless period I watched the sun slowly sinking toward the sea. A light, warm breeze was blowing off the land. Seagulls drifted across the orange-colored sky. The tiny waves gently broke onto the sand. And within me there was a sense of contentedness, which sometimes envelops me for no apparent reason.

After the sun had set and I had started back to my car, the peace began to deepen. As I strolled along the sand I began to feel myself release. It was as if everything inside—muscles, viscera, bones—began to let go. And as my body let go, the mind began to cease and desist. A transition that I could feel was now beginning to occur, and I knew it was important to keep from thinking, to keep totally out of the way.

Now I became aware of a movement of change taking place. It was as if the life that I felt in the body was passing out of the body. As this was happening I began to feel myself leaving this world and emerging into a dif-

ferent universe, a universe vast and infinite and ex-
cruciatingly beautiful. *It was*—a universe filled with joy
and love. And there I was walking—at least the body
was. And there I was outside my body living in a joyous
sense of life. This was real. It wasn't a fantasy or fiction.
It was real beyond all doubt, much more real than
earthly life. In a strange, inexplicable way this experience *was* truth. It *was* love. It *was* God.

While making my way up the embankment to the car,
I looked up at the moon in the cloudless sky from my
new vantage in this new universe. How much more
beautiful the moon and sky were from this place. How
much more beautiful things were from this place.
Everything about took on a radiance of beauty—the
street lights, the shadowy shapes of trees, the couple
hugging in the parking lot, even the shape of the car was
beautiful.

I didn't consider analyzing what was happening. It
was important not to. It was important that the mind
and body, which surely could be activated again by
thought, remain out of the experience. And they were. It
felt as if they were stunned by the magnitude and power
of the energy within the experience.

All the way home it went on. And then all through
the evening the essence of it was there. Sitting before the
window watching the flickering stars, I could feel myself
as light and transparent as the breeze. I wondered if at
this moment anyone could actually see me? Yet I could
look down at the hands, the legs, the body and see that
they were still there. And yet was I really there or here,
or was I somewhere else, somewhere so different from
this physical universe?

I slept lightly that night. To fall into a deep sleep
would cause the experience to end. All through the night
it continued. And then toward morning I lost con-

sciousness. When I awoke the depth of awareness of living in this new universe had diminished, but its glow lingered on.

Is there a God-self? I asked this question early this morning as I sat on the bank of a pond feeling that beautiful, lightening energy of love. I wondered if what I was feeling was my other self, a self not of matter but of Spirit. My intuition, insight, perception said yes, there really was another self. Whether we call it a God-self or a spiritual identity or use any other words isn't important. What is important is that one can feel, almost see, this other self in operation, opposed to the matter self.

I asked from this higher vantage: Why the human being and from whence do we come? The perception which arose again was that this matter-entity is not real—not real in the sense of being part of this other perfect and eternal life I was experiencing. What the human is, is a figment of a false assumption which we imagine to be true. It's a dream of sorts, a dream which has several strong witnesses as to the truth of the dream's existence.

These witnesses—the five human senses and the material-based mind—attest that the dream is not only true but is the only reality. But I feel the reality of our spiritual identity is the only truth about ourselves. This reality is not to be found in the sense dream; it can't be, since the senses and mind can't comprehend our spiritual identity or Spirit. But our spiritual identity which participates with Spirit can comprehend the senses and mind and enter into them to change them, so that eventually we begin to awaken from the dream. And when we fully awaken, the dream shall be no more. At that time we shall come into the fullness of who we really are—a being of God having all the qualities of God.

What good does it do me to believe that I have a spiritual identity? Perhaps it might help to shift my attention from who I'm not to who I am. It also might remove some fear about the body's death, for I might more deeply realize that my demise won't destroy my real identity.

But belief is not the same as experiencing the truth of who I actually am, for belief is a thing of the mind; it is a thing associated with the dream part of myself. And though I may receive comfort and perhaps security from my beliefs, I see I must go further and find out the truth for myself. I must not take anyone's word for it.

Truth, Spirit, is felt as I die to self, for I can see that the human, mortal self isn't my eternal identity, nor is it connected to eternal Spirit. If it were, I'd be experiencing eternity and deathlessness right now.

So this morning for me there was a death of the self, with all its thoughts and feelings. Now what was partially hidden—Spirit and my deep connection to Spirit became fully evident.

Sunday, September 18

Today on a walk through the woods I came across a newly fallen tree. As I stood by the tree peering at those gigantic roots torn from the earth, I looked up to where the tree had stood. Suddenly and spontaneously, I perceived another tree standing there in all its eternality, beauty, and splendor. It was a tree which material eyes could not see. Was this an imagining of mine? Surely from the human way of seeing things it was. But right

51

then, at that moment, I was perceiving a "real" tree, through feeling the depths and breadth of the energy of Spirit. Thus I was realizing the real substantialness of Spirit. From this basis I saw a tree that was as eternal as God's eternity. And as I saw that tree as eternal, I saw myself and all other human beings and creatures—everything on earth—as eternal.

"So what is true," I asked while standing next to the 'dead tree,' "the human way of seeing things or Spirit's?"

Monday, September 19

He said that in his estimation Spirit and spiritual things aren't real. Matter is real. Human love is real. Pleasure and happiness are real, as well as sickness and death. But this thing of Spirit and feeling a love, an energy, coming from Spirit is poppycock; it is a delusion of the mind; it is wishful thinking projected out to create an experience called Spirit.

But how could it be a delusion of the mind when the mind isn't involved in the experience? Neither is the body, for that matter. Still, I know the problem this man faces. Not having experienced Spirit, he must be skeptical. It's important that he be so, for to accept what I or anyone says without testing things out for himself is to become a follower of other's experiences and concepts rather than being a person with a light within himself.

I hope that someday he will experience the energy of Spirit. Then the doubt of Spirit's existence will disappear.

Wednesday, September 21

The beach was magical this morning. Everything looked crisp, fresh and clear. The sea gulls' white feathers

52

shone in the sun. The ocean, greenish-blue and dazzling with light, stretched out and met the cobalt-colored sky. The thousands of white-washed shells at the water's edge bounced gently along the sand with each surge of the waves. Everything one looked at, everywhere one look-ed, one found a richness of life; a sense of fullness of joy, a sense of freedom.

Surely love is sensed in freedom and in quietness, when one is alert and awake to everything around. And then the sensing of love simply begins to happen. For no particular reason, love is there in the richness of joy.

Saturday, October 1

This morning while sitting on a sunny slope in the mountains that incredible leavening of love began to happen. It felt as if my whole body was lightening and there was a kneading process going on within the body's sensations. The kneading occurs, I feel, because the energy seems to be changing the body to become more like itself.

After awhile I began to feel that I was being lifted up above the earth and into another sphere; a sphere where there was no matter-feeling, no body to weigh me down and hold me. The thought occurred: Why couldn't the energy just leaven away everything which one feels of matter, leaven away the bodily feelings specifically which keep us so fixed and imprisoned within the body.

The leavening with its lightness and upliftingness kept on. It grew stronger and brought me higher above the earth and all earthly feelings. I could see the hawks circling in the sky above but I felt totally unrelated to these things. They were of a different realm. I had been raised up. And though I could perceive everything about, I was not part of these things.

Monday, October 3

Unless I'm aware of the mind and its activities—its thoughts and feelings—then I can find myself caught up in the smallest and silliest issues. Little insignificant thoughts can keep jumping up and distracting me. And the mind, just as though it's being drawn by a magnet, thinks about these thoughts and doesn't wake up to the fact that it has been thinking about them until the damage has been done—the damage of being drawn into a totally self-conscious state without realizing it.

To be aware of the mind requires that I watch the mind's thoughts without judging them, for if I do judge then I'm not really seeing the mind in the actual way it works. Instead I'm superimposing on the mind what I think it should be and should think. Then there's no freedom from this me who judges.

It's when there's freedom from the judger—myself—
that the life of Spirit can grow, deepen, become full.

Saturday, October 8

Krishnamurti has said that thought is matter. I'd like
to put it differently. When we feel ourselves materially
then we think material thoughts, for matter is our base,
the seeming essence of our being.

Conversely, when we feel ourselves spiritually—as
part of the energy of Spirit—then our thinking becomes
more spiritual because Spirit is our base, the essence of
our being.

So what is true, Spirit or matter? The world would
answer matter for this is the sense that most people feel.
But when one begins to feel one's matter sensations,
when yielded, being replaced by the feelings of Spirit's
energy then one knows that Spirit is the real truth—the
truth of our being now, before we were born, and
forevermore.

Is the body just a piece of matter, or is the body a
material formation of the human mind—this mind whose
essence and character emanates from a material sense of
the physical universe? If the latter is the case, and I feel
that it is, then the bodily senses we feel must be part of
this material mind. So it follows that if we are to heal
the body we need to heal the mind's assumption or
belief in the body's materiality. We do this through having the mind/body feel the energy of Spirit.

To realize that the body is part of the human mind
can be a great help in healing, for when we direct the
energy to the body we are aware that it's not matter
we're directing to. Rather, it's the person's material-

feeling mentality—it's the human, physical sense of one's self. Thus when Spirit touches what we call the senses, the person begins to be aware that he can yield these senses to the energy. And as he does a healing naturally takes place.

Thursday, October 13

We had gone to the mountains and eaten lunch on a sunny slope five thousand feet above a valley. Off to our left were two lakes, postage stamp size from our vantage point, but which were large bodies of water where in the summer people come to boat, fish, and swim. It was unusually warm for this time of year. The sun penetrated our bodies through our light clothing.

After lunch the three of us [Caroline, Letitia and John] took hikes alone. We made plans to meet back at our luncheon-point in about an hour.

After walking down a slope for a while, I found a sunny, solitary rock to sit on which offered a different angle of the valley. The silence here was immense; not a sound, other than nature's, could be heard. A tall redwood, beautiful, straight, majestic, stood twenty feet ahead. Its branches created a silhouette against the steel-blue sky. A dozen feet ahead, nestled in the ground, was a clump of grass with yellow flowers peeking up.

I had been watching the flowers swaying in the light breeze for quite a while. I had also been watching my thoughts as impassively as I was watching the flowers. Suddenly all thoughts were gone, and with this the image of myself disappeared. For this moment without time I had no memory of any prior existence here on earth. I had no recollection of past, present, or future. Everything was now. And yet now wasn't even recognized as now. What was discernible was an infinitude which was growing. It felt as if this immenseness was expanding in the head—before the head, behind it, around it. And the immenseness was substantial; it wasn't vaporous or "spiritual." It was as substantial as what we call matter, but unlike matter it was totally harmonious, totally perfect. It was total love.

There was a realization that this immense, loving, substantialness which was expanding everywhere *was* Spirit. However, unlike the way I most often feel Spirit, which is in the body, this was in the head. It was felt in the head because all thought and mental image of myself were gone. Thus Spirit had replaced that which was dead. The energy and life of Spirit had replaced the energy and life of self-consciousness. Life had replaced death. What was true had replaced what was a dream. And now there was an experiencing of eternal life; a life without a beginning or an ending; a life which had never been created and thus could never die. It simply was. And this wasness, this isness, was everything. It was and is the only truth. Everything else in the temporal world was and is unreal.

Spirit is all I've desired most of my life. It's all I ever felt before I came here. And it's all I'll ever feel when I leave here. Spirit is life. Thus Spirit is the life of everyone. To know this we have only to feel it.

Love flourishes in freedom; it flourishes in the freedom where nothing is pressuring one, where thought is quiet, where desires, hopes, and worries are gone. Then we can just look and enjoy and commune and love. We can be simply as we are—a being of Spirit.

Tuesday, October 18

Awhile ago a professor at a university back east wrote me and sent along several books written by his guru. In his letter he explained that he felt that finding God could be accomplished only after a "long spiritual ascent." Thus it was important that we find the "true teacher" and listen and follow him. (He had read both our books so he certainly knew that I didn't feel this way.)

Since he was so forthright, I felt I could be too and not spend time mincing words. So I wrote him that I thought that God, Spirit, was found in the now or not at all. For, I asked, how can the eternal be found through the process of time which the "long spiritual ascent" implies? Eternity and time can never meet, despite the belief that through evolving we'll eventually get to the eternal. For us to experience the eternal, time must stop, which means that we must let go of our time-based minds and lives.

I also wrote—gently, I hope—that perhaps, just perhaps, his guru wasn't the true teacher. Then what? Does one spend years and decades studying the words of someone only to discover that it's all been for naught. For me, I said, the search for Spirit must be done humbly and without knowing what the truth is. Then perhaps that which is true beyond all humans' or gurus' truths will reveal itself to us.

I suppose I made my point, but evidently I didn't make a friend, for I've not heard a word from him since my letter.

If someone is going north and I'm going south, then I suppose we never will meet unless one of us changes direction.

Thursday, October 20

You sit in the sickroom of a man you're trying to help. You look down at the emaciated face and the eyes

58

staring straight ahead. The ravages of the sickness have taken their toll.

Everyone believes in and fears cancer. Because of the severity of the belief and the tremendous fear attached to the idea, image, and word *cancer*, this disease has become a scourge as frightening as the Black Plague. So it's important not to become impressed by the physical appearance. It's important to see this man as a being of Spirit. In that dimension he's perfect and whole.

You reach down and take his cold hand. He looks up through mesmerized eyes and tries to smile. You tell him that you're going to work for him by sending the energy of love to him. You tell him love can heal his body. It has healed so many others and it can heal him. You tell him also that it's all right if he falls asleep, or if he wants to talk that's O.K. too.

You go over and sit in the chair at the foot of his bed and begin to direct the energy you feel toward him. At first you close your eyes so you can sense that other dimension more easily and deeply. Later, after working for perhaps ten minutes, you open your eyes and watch the feeble body and the feeble breathing. His breathing appears to be more regular now. On the currents of the energy, you tell him silently that he has nothing to fear for Spirit truly is with him. He is part of Spirit and Spirit is part of him. That's the true essence of his real being. And this being is sickless and deathless.

You recall Jesus' words: "Be not afraid. I am with you always." Be not afraid, dear man, for Spirit's healing energy is with you always. You realize how important it is to remove the fear. And there is plenty of fear here. There's fear from his family that he's getting weaker. There's fear that the situation is hopeless. There's the fear that the pain will increase. There's the stark fear of death which you feel each time you enter the room.

You continue working. You again think of Jesus and what he said about angels coming to minister unto one.

You don't believe in angels, but why shouldn't you? Why should the whole thing about angels be so outlandish? Maybe there really are angels, and maybe they can really help this man. You look at his face and realize again that this emaciated physical body isn't the true person. You know this is the case for yourself, thus you can know and feel it is so for this man. This is not self-deception. It is true. It's a far greater truth than the supposed truths of matter and matter life.

You go over once more to his bed. He opens his eyes, reaches for your hand, and says in that raspy, weak voice, "Thank you. I felt it." You leave, drive to a solitary meadow, and begin walking. All the while you continue sending him the energy from Spirit.

Saturday, October 22

You close your eyes, let go of all material sensations, and enter that vast infinitude where Spirit abides. Here, there are no disharmonies—no time, no sorrow, no pain, no fear, no death. Here all is perfect and at peace. To live here eternally with Eternity while one is still on earth is the challenge and the work.

You open your eyes and see imperfection and limitations all about. Everything—the ocean, the houses, the birds, the people—speaks of temporality. And in these things is disharmony, pain, and suffering. It must be so, for deeply all these things of time and matter are unreal—they are illusory, for only the eternity of Spirit is real.

Sunday, October 23

I look about in this vast, horrendous, beautiful, brutal world and see insecurity everywhere. I see that one day

I can be feeling alive and well and the next day I could be deathly ill; or I could have suffered an accident; or I could even be dead, or if not me, then one of my loved ones.

And from these insecurities—from these fears that my happiness might soon be smashed—I look all about and cry, "Where is there something lasting and true that I can hold on to? Where can I find a lasting sense of peace and happiness? How can I know that after I die, after my loved ones die, that we'll all live on."

The voice of this religion or that religion eventually answers my cry with: "The security, happiness, truth and immortality you're seeking is found with my creed, with my dogma, with my doctrine, with my church. The knowing you want is found with the knowledge and experience of our religion's founder." I utter a sigh of relief for what I've been looking for has finally been found. Now I can stop fretting, stop fearing. Now I can be assured that every exigency of life will be met and that someday I'll be in heaven with God and with all my loved ones. I feel good about this, I feel absolutely confident that finally I have found the right answer, the right way, the only way. And I'm gratified that so many other people believe the same as I do, for there's a great feeling of comfort in being with people of similar beliefs.

Someday, however, maybe years down the line, life may force me to reopen my mind and look at things anew. Then I may start to requestion my beliefs, requestion my "knowledge," requestion whether any religious creed or doctrine can give me that deep, rich, full sense of being which is the truth of myself and which is really the truth and security which I've always been seeking.

Monday, October 24

The material sense of life is a cover-up—an attempt to

cloak the real life of Spirit. Thus it's the only evil there is. And we, living on planet Earth, feel only this material sense so much of the time. Is it any wonder that our lives are so difficult?

I can feel the depths of the energy and find the distance between myself and everything else diminish or disappear. At these times I feel I'm part of what I'm looking at; I'm part of the ocean, of the tree, of the flower; I'm participating in and with everything I see.

At other times when feeling the energy deeply, I look about and feel my being distinct and apart from everything around. At these times, it feels as if I'm viewing life from another dimension, which in fact I am. Thus, being separate or apart from the world, I'm in a state of nonreaction toward the world; the world and the things therein aren't a concern to me because my life and being are in another sphere.

Why these changes in perception? The reason can be found in my inclination toward the world at the time I'm feeling the energy. If I'm concerned and interested in the world of flowers, sea, trees, and people, then the feeling of the energy naturally puts me in communion with everything. If I'm not interested in the world at the moment or feel the need to get lost for awhile, then immersion in the other dimension brings about a sense of being separate from the world. In either case it is Spirit that is real.

Wednesday, October 26

Had a beautiful walk this morning. The sun was bright, the meadows and woods were alive with sounds. Even the toot of a truck's horn from the highway several miles away sounded like a song.

To hear and see from all angles at once—to see and hear, not from one perspective or from one part of one's being, but from everywhere, from a totality of one's being. This is joy. This is emptiness of self. This is the fullness of love.

There was love this morning on my walk, not the love of the day or of nature, but a love coming from that other dimension which filled all nature and my heart.

Thursday, October 27

What is the one quality which will allow us to feel Spirit immediately without any technique, thought, or time involved? If there were such a quality, then perhaps thousands or even millions of people might learn that this life and energy of Spirit is real.

I've talked and written so much about yielding the body and the mind and of needing humility to feel Spirit, but it's evident that not too many people can do this, especially at first. So as I was sitting by a pond this morning and feeling an immense amount of Spirit, I wondered what will allow the ordinary person to feel Spirit's life. For after all the life of Spirit, because it is real, should be more widely felt than it presently is.

The answer came right from the heart of feeling the energy: We can all raise our life above the consideration, the thoughts, the sensations of matter, for this is what keeps us entangled in matter's life and thus unable to feel Spirit's life. So while we're looking at a bird or the sky or a pond, if we can just raise our material-based mind above these things, then we'll enter easily and naturally into that Timeless Haven where everything can be seen from Spirit's vantage.

It's very helpful to realize matter is a low-energy state

of consciousness, while Spirit's state of life is above and beyond this low-energy field. Thus to find this life of Spirit, one must have or develop an intensity within, which will allow one to ascend above matter's life and enter into that domain where Spirit dwells.

He said that he always thought that God was simply a higher state of consciousness. I said that I didn't consider God as a state of consciousness. This implies that the human mind has some affinity or kinship with God or Spirit and can, through study, learning, discipline, meditation, somehow raise itself up into the consciousness of God.

I consider God as a state of life which we can enter when we have found a way to leave the consciousness of matter, which is really the consciousness of the human mind.

Saturday, October 29

While asleep I may dream I'm having a conversation with a particular person. Then suddenly the scene shifts and I'm talking to someone else, or perhaps I'm running along a beach, or I find myself in some strange situation. This sudden change from one place to another, from one situation to another, which is totally illogical from a waking state, doesn't seem illogical at all from a dream state. In fact, it's quite logical. It's only when I awake and find myself once more in the world's logic system that I look back at my dream and see what a fantasy it was.

So now, while wide awake and feeling the energy, I look about me and see people, birds, animals—all forms of matter—moving, flying, walking, running throughout the world, and I ask: How can matter be animated? It's totally illogical that something as dead and inert as matter could come to life. And yet it appears that it has.

Then I go a bit further in my questioning and ask: What could be more illogical than a nerve feeling, or taste buds tasting, or eyes seeing? (Or is it the brain that sees, according to present-day science? If so, this is also very illogical.) And what about this piece of matter called the brain? Do I actually believe that it can think? Or that an organ called a stomach could be upset and report that upset to the brain.

In the midst of asking these questions I begin to wonder if someday science might examine these "logical" issues of life. Perhaps if it did, and declared such things illogical and illusory, we'd all begin to perceive a bit better that what we've assumed, supposed, and believed to be laws of matter are no such thing at all. With this discovery, I'm sure we would begin to realize that we have more freedom from matter than we ever dreamed possible.

It's only when we feel that ultralogical world of Spirit that we begin to doubt deeply the logic of this world.

Wednesday, November 2

May Sarton* has written that many of her friends almost constantly have to deal with pain, bitterness, fear, anger, guilt, loneliness, despair. These states of mind and emotions, she said, often send them into deep depressions.

I'm reminded of what a noted psychiatrist said recently. He stated that the normal human being could expect to go through a day or two of depression about once

---

*American author.

every month. And, he added, we could expect to go through longer periods of depression—periods up to a week or more—once or twice a year.

Our recurrent depressions couldn't be the result of life-altering situations such as a death in the family or a terminal illness. These situations occur far too infrequently. So our depressions must come from another source. Could it be that they're triggered simply by a *feeling*? The feeling could be as benign as listlessness, or lack of energy. If, however, this feeling isn't changed or isn't alleviated, then it's liable to grow in our consciousness. Thus the mind becomes concerned, agitated; it worries, it frets; it begins to think about the unhappy times in our life—the time when our son died, the times when someone hurt us deeply, the times when we felt inadequate, worthless.

Now with these thoughts tugging at us, we naturally begin to mull, to stew—we begin to reconstruct piece by piece every detail of our past unhappinesses and sense exactly what our feelings were during those times. We start to worry about something similar happening to us again. So now we find ourselves really in a fix, a fix caused not by our present circumstances but by the myth of what might be. What might be now becomes our present concern, our present reality. And though we may perceive that we're dealing with phantoms and ghosts which have no present relevance, we still find ourselves caught in the miasma of dark thoughts and feelings, which is the essence and cause of depression.

Illness, I've found, occurs in a similar way. For example, first I have a slight feeling of an upset stomach, a stuffy nose, a pain in the body. Then thought looks about trying to find a cause for these feelings, which it will likely call the flu, a cold, or whatever. And, lo and behold, if I don't find a way to get rid of the feelings, and thus the thoughts and concerns about the feelings, then I'll probably end up being sick.

So what can one do to destroy these sensations? I've found that it's important to deal with negatives when they first arise; otherwise they might grow into undue proportions. A neighbor recently told me that when she first begins to feel sick she takes a long swim in her pool. This seems to work for her. I also know of a professional athlete who goes out for a long run when he feels a cold or the flu coming on. He maintains that going to bed only makes him feel worse, whereas running makes him feel robust and healthy.

When I feel the first sign of something wrong, I go after the feeling with the energy of Spirit. And, I find, if I've caught the feeling soon enough, then every adverse sensation will soon be gone. The marvelous thing about working things out with the energy is that afterwards I'm not just back to a normal state of health and wellbeing. Rather, I'm experiencing a transcendence of self and living more deeply in that realm of joy.

Thursday, November 3

Just watched on television a famous old movie star break down and weep as he read one of his poems about growing old. He was experiencing the hardship and pain of having to live so long.

I read a story in the newspaper this evening about a twenty-five year old man who has terminal cancer and is fighting as hard as he can to stay alive. He was faced with the hardship and pain of having to die too soon.

What kind of world do we have here? We see, if we've lived long enough to have suffered some ourselves, that we have a world of imperfection. Here in the world of matter nothing is perfect; here all is filled with temporary happiness, occasional joy, and then eventual pain, suffering, and death.

Seeing this dilemma as a young man, I asked if there is anything beyond this world which is real, which is absolute, which is perhaps perfect, which was perhaps made by a creator or a Creator with supreme intelligence. I found by opening up my being to this possibility that indeed there is another Reality beyond matter, a Reality incredibly greater than I ever could have thought or imagined.* I was shown, too, that within this Reality—really the essence of this Reality—is eternity, which is different from immortality. Whereas immortality implies continuity of existence, eternity is without any sense of time.

Not only is this Reality a timeless life, it is in every regard a life opposite to matter's life. This other life or Reality is perfect, joyous, deathless, ageless, sickless. Everything is perfect there. So it was natural to want to be in touch with it. More than touch it, I wanted to feel that life fully and live with it if possible. And I knew it was possible because it is real, it is a living, pulsating, infinite life.

So, over the years, I sought ways to be with that life. And I found that I could be with it when I had to some extent died to my matter-sensing existence. This was understandable, for when I was filled with matter-feelings, with matter-thoughts, with material drives and pullings, then there was no room for the other life to be with me.

All these things I recalled as I watched the old movie star and thought about the young man with cancer. My heart goes out to them. How hard it is to live on earth

---

*At about the age of twenty-three John had an experience which he says showed him the validity of this other Reality. This experience is described more fully in *Conversations in Spirit*.

without this other energy of life. Even with the energy at times it's hard.

Considering the young man with cancer, I ask why so many doctors think they must tell patients that they're going to die or not recover fully. Unless a patient demands to know the hard medical "facts," then I think it's unwise to say these things, for not only have I seen, heard, and experienced the untold harm such informing does, but no one, not even the most renowned physician, can be absolutely sure of the prognosis. This is confirmed by the tens of thousands of people who have recovered from "terminal" illnesses and "totally disabling" accidents.

The several times I was in the hospital and diagnosed as being seriously ill, a more positive outlook by the doctors, rather than their dire predictions, would have helped my mental outlook immensely. This in turn would have projected, I'm sure, onto my body and helped me to recover. Instead the doctors essentially gave me up.

The first time, a doctor told my friends that they had better pray that I *didn't* recover because if I lived I would have severe brain damage and would be like a vegetable!

The second time an eminent neurologist stood at the foot of my bed and told me I'd never walk again. I might be able to hobble along with a walker or a pair of canes if I got lucky, but I'd certainly never have the full use of my legs again.

A third time the medical prognosis was six months to live. The ensuing months were a tremendous struggle for me. But with immense help from Spirit, the prognosis was again proved wrong.

It's interesting to reflect that each healing came about nonmedically. When I was in a coma, I just woke up.

No one knows why. When I was paralyzed, I used my knowledge of yoga to help heal myself. Then with the cancer Spirit's energy healed my body.

So my position is: When one is confronted with a dire medical diagnosis and prognosis, then look for alternative forms of healing. If we believe in medicine and wish to stick with the medical people, fine. But if we're led to try something different then we ought to feel free to do so. Things other than medicine can work. This is understandable when we realize how much the body is affected by the mind, and even more so when we realize how much Spirit's energy can change the body.

Awhile ago I visited a patient diagnosed as having terminal cancer. When I told her about my overcoming cancer, she just looked at me sadly and shook her head. "But it's useless," she said. "The doctors have told me that I'm going to die."

It wasn't long before she was gone.

Shuffling along the hospital corridors with my walker,* I'd look into the dozens of rooms and see those dozens of different faces and bodies. How many of them were contorted by suffering. How many of those lonely, despairing faces had tubes coming out of their noses and stomachs, their arms and legs. And there they lay enduring, hoping, waiting, sleeping.

We lucky ones made it home. For a while everything might be all right, our health and happiness might remain intact. And yet, I used to think, each one of us waits for our next episode with sickness, accident, and possible death. Though we might try to avoid thinking about such things, the images, filled with fear, come in to haunt us in our weaker moments. What a life this is!

---

*In 1965 John's lower body was partially paralyzed.

How vulnerable we are to life's whims, to life's fates. How helpless we are to ward off our attackers, our destroyers.

My stay in the hospital served me well. It was a time I needed to observe, to ponder, and to consider what is important in life. It was a time to realize my own mortality, my own limited time on earth. I thought of my brother who had died just a year earlier. He was only thirty-six and so strong and healthy until the cancer struck. All these considerings made me conclude that if I am going to accomplish anything of worth, then I had better get started immediately.

I can still hear the voice of the woman in the room next to mine. Every night she'd begin moaning and then crying out and then shrieking that she didn't want to die here, that she wanted to go home. Her cries sent chills throughout the hospital. You not only felt her anguish but you saw yourself someday in her place. She was no different from any of us. It was only that her time had come and ours hadn't yet arrived.

Night after night the poor, dear soul kept pleading with the nurses. Why didn't any of her relatives or friends take her home? Couldn't they understand that she didn't want to spend her last days on earth within the stark white walls and the antiseptic environment of a hospital.

Then one night there was no more cries or shrieks.

Friday, November 4

Several of us took a lunch and went into the hills behind Ojai. The stream we sat by was bordered with smooth white boulders which shimmered in the heat.

The shade of the trees and the coolness of the water were welcome on this hot, dry day. Everything about seemed to reflect the sun and the heat making everything sparkle with a translucent light. At times like these I feel matter and Spirit are somehow intertwined.

How different we are, my friends and I. Their education and experience convinces them that "reality" can be found only through learning and knowledge which is of the mind. My education and experience convinces me that reality is found only through direct experience, which for me is above and beyond learning and knowledge. For them, my way is too altruistic and not germane to the world we live in. For me, their way is too matter-of-fact, too intellectual.

As we talked today, I attempted at various times to get them to feel what I was feeling. And they tried at various times to get me to understand what they were thinking. Both they and I were somewhat successful, but not totally. That would be impossible because we're different. Yet despite our differences we care for each other. We understand each other. We really love each other. And maybe that's the whole point. Maybe that's what relationships are all about.

Sunday, November 6

You look out at nature and see a bird, a tree, the clouds, and you realize that there's a distance between you and these things—a distance that creates a sense of conflict because there is no communing, no harmony, no love between you and them. So the distance is closed by your simple awareness of the space between you and these things. Now there is love stirring and the movement of joy and a communing with everything about.

You look within and you find there's a distance between yourself and you're thoughts, between yourself and your feelings. In this perception is the closing of the distance. Whereas a moment before there were you and your thoughts and feelings now there is only a rich, full sense of being. Whereas before there was conflict and a sense of disharmony, now there is peace and contentedness. And in this peace and contentedness is love and Spirit.

Monday, November 7

In the deep yielding of the body—the yielding of one's whole internal feelings to Spirit—is the deepening with Spirit. To yield in this way without any sense of self-consciousness or self-will begins "the transition" which is the changing from self-conscious life into a life full of Spirit.

It was so easy to do this today—so simple, so utterly unself-conscious. What came of it was a walker walking totally with the energy of Spirit. I wondered again why I couldn't just lift off the earth—lift off this mesmeric, self-conscious, gravitational-pulling, negative-energized world. Perhaps someday I will.

While on a walk this morning, I considered the question of why one could feel Spirit's energy quite deeply and still have human sensations going on within the body. The question was: What keeps these bodily sensations alive? I saw that it was human will and action emanating from this will which keep me alive in the world. Without will and will's action these feelings would dissolve and disappear.

I looked within and felt several uncomfortable physical sensations within the body. So I gave up the tightness of will, first in my face, and I felt this whole area let go. Then I gave up the tension of will throughout my body and felt the body let go. Now there was the feeling of an empowering by the energy, everywhere. The body's sensations were actually changing. I could feel it happening and with the change a strengthening, a solidifying, was occurring.

The process continued until I began to think of something quite irrelevant. With thought now operating, I began to feel some human sensations returning. I let go again of human will created by thought. Once more I felt the sensations of will being transformed by the energy of Spirit.

It was a marvelous relearning to watch this process and to see how will created by thought produces the sensations which keep us entrenched in the world.

Wednesday, November 9

In the middle of the night a fever arose. I worked

75

against it with the energy until the symptoms were alleviated and then I fell back to sleep. When I awakened I was greeted with a high temperature and an aching body. Once more I began working, but this time the symptoms held on. In fact, I had to work vigorously just to hold things at bay.

In the afternoon, still in pain and dragged out, I got in the car and drove to an isolated stretch of beach. Each step along the sand was a struggle because of the pain in my head and spine and the general feeling of listlessness. After a while, as I was pondering what was keeping these feelings going, it suddenly occurred to me that the energy causing the pain needed to be drained away. This, I remembered, was the way I had often dealt with the cancer.

So I began working at letting go of the body, especially in those places where it hurt the most. Simultaneously, I tried to let the pain and the fever sensation just drain from my body, like one would drain water from a pipe. After a while I began to sense a breakthrough. Now I worked even harder. And as I did I could feel the discomfort being alleviated. A blessed sense of wholeness and harmony was slowly returning. The fever and pain were gradually subsiding. By the time I had driven home, I was feeling much better. By evening I was well.

Through letting go and draining away the body's energy, one feels a natural infilling of Spirit's energy. It's as if Spirit is waiting to enter us, when our lives—our wills and energy systems—have diminished.

Friday, November 11

I remember when feeling so very ill with the cancer that I'd often force myself to get out of bed and go out for a walk. How terrible I used to feel at the beginning of the walk. And how buoyantly joyous I'd often feel by the time I was back home. This buoyancy came from letting go entirely of my bodily life. With this letting go there was an infilling of that other life—that eternal, harmonious life of Spirit.

I remember too how many times I would sit in the hills after feeling the depths of the energy and realize that it didn't matter whether I lived or died, for only Spirit's life was really going on. So if the self-conscious image which the world calls me "dies" or disappears, it would all be the same. I would still be alive and living within that life. That life is forever and because of it, I am forever.

Just been rereading the *Phaedo* (a dialogue about Socrates' death.) It's amazing to see how differently I used to read Plato's words fifteen or twenty years ago. Back then I never fully perceived Socrates' view of the body. He thought the body interferes with the soul's pure perception of truth. He stated that the lover of wisdom, who is the true philosopher, dies daily to the body. This is imperative, he felt, for the soul must be freed from its bodily prison of the senses—freed from this disturber of the soul's contemplations of truth.

Because of his feelings about the body, Socrates didn't fear drinking the hemlock, for he believed that through death the soul would finally be unfettered to once again roam the infinite realm of truth.

The soul—the being of the person—can be free to a tremendous extent, right here and now, to roam unfettered in that infinite realm. What it requires is being in contact with Spirit. Surely Spirit, God, Truth is that life we will experience and live in after death. So why not now? Why wait?

I recall those many days I spent in my youth wandering the hundreds of acres of solitary woods behind our small summer cottage. How alive I felt. Every sense was alert to the faintest sound and the slightest sight. I felt adventure awaiting at every turn—along every path, behind every tree, by every water's edge. Always there was something new to be discovered—a toad squatting in some reeds, a turtle sunning on a lily pad, a deer or a bobcat being startled and startling me. And how I scrutinized the ground looking for a mound where I just knew an Indian of long ago lay buried.

I did find an arrowhead once. At least I think it was an arrowhead. I really couldn't tell for sure because time had ground away the stone. But it was great fun to think that some Indian had once shot his arrow with this arrowhead. Perhaps he had killed a deer to feed his family, or maybe he had shot a bear. Later I discovered there were no bears around, but it was exciting imagining that there were.

It was a peak time, those days of my youth, a time when I felt a lot of the energy, a lot of God. If someone had asked me then to describe what I felt, I suppose I would have answered that I just felt good, that I just felt that life was an adventure, that I just felt life was a constant opening into a new life.

I remember when dad bought my older brother and me twenty-two caliber rifles. We practiced daily with targets until we got to be very good shots. Then one day we took to the woods with our rifles. Like so many kids, we were innocently looking about for a moving target to shoot at. We didn't really think about hurting anything; we just wanted to test out our shooting skills.

Along the way we saw a squirrel high up in a tree.

There was no way we could ever hit that squirrel for he was so far away and moving so fast across the branches. Raising our guns together, we shot in the squirrel's direction. To our surprise and shock the squirrel was knocked off the branch and began falling the hundred or so feet to the ground, bouncing off branches all the way down.

We ran over to the lifeless body. A bullet had taken off part of its head. It was such a horror to see that innocent thing who had been alive and happily playing in the tree a moment before. My brother started to cry. It was so unlike him to cry. He was always so strong, it seemed. I looked down again at the squirrel. I began to cry too. Then I started to run. I ran until I got back to the cottage where I told my parents what had happened. They seemed to think that what we had done was all right, and that made me feel a little better.

I went outside to wait for my brother. After a while I saw him coming down the dirt road. He was holding the dead squirrel by the tail and crying his heart out. "Get me a shovel," he said in between sobs. "I want to bury it right here outside my bedroom window."

That small childhood episode made such an impression on my brother and me that we never shot at another living thing ever again. The horror of killing anything stayed with us all through our lives.

I remember, too, when I was a child, all those times that I found myself removed from life, perhaps in another room a little way off from the noise of parents, grandparents and other people. I felt a sense of joy in being apart. I sensed then that my being was distinct, solid, intact, and far removed from those whom I was daily involved with.

Sometimes I'd spend minutes just listening to those far

away voices, all the while feeling that sense of mystery which comes from being removed, alone, apart from life. These were some of the first sensings of the energy that I can recall. Perhaps these times created the impetus for desiring to live with Spirit. How far afield I got before finding my way back!

Tuesday, November 15

When one looks at anything—the ocean, the trees, the mountains, one's grief, sorrow, pain, happiness—with one's mind, one's eyes, one's ears, one's heart, one's body, one's being then there's a breaking through the energy of ego which brings about an egoless state. And from this vantage point of egoless being there is freedom—freedom to look, to commune, to be, to participate with everything about.

This morning it was this way. As I drove along the sunlit road there was a father lifting a child on a swing. There was a mother leaning on the fence of a corral, talking to another child. There were squirrels scurrying across the road and an arbor formed over the road by the trees' arching branches. There was the sunlight glittering off the leaves, and there were the mountains in the background whose peaks were reaching up to touch the clouds. There were several dozen steer standing woefully in a field, waiting to be shipped off to market. There was a sparkling stream flowing by the side of the road.

When I stopped the car and walked down by the stream and sat a while, I saw the hundreds of spiders on the face of the water, pushing and shoving each other as they waited for a morsel of food to be brought to them.

All these things were seen without an ego to interfere,

identify, or interpret the seeing. And in this seeing were freedom and joy. There was Spirit.

Friday, November 18

It's strange and beautiful to watch oneself—one's speakings and actions—as one would watch another person. To be at that proper distance from one's self, so that all one does can be seen clearly, is freedom from self. In this detachment from self is found a sense of space, a sense of inner emptiness of all thoughts and sensations.

So what is watching whom? Is it that our eternal beinghood is watching the temporal person as he walks along, speaks, and acts? I believe it is. It feels this way.

Saturday, November 19

Been reading the book: *Great People of the Bible*. And again I'm appalled at the terror and atrocities which have been perpetrated against humanity in the name of God and religion. All through history men have been killing each other to preserve and protect their creeds and doctrines, to preserve and protect their religious heritages, to preserve and protect their power status.

I just got through reading about one of humanity's more vicious acts. God, so the story goes, told a famous lawgiver that Canaan was to be the Promised Land. The only problem was that there were thousands of Canaanites living in the land. This, however, didn't deter the dedicated for they went in and slaughtered every man, woman, child, and even babies and animals. Nothing was left alive, for Jehovah's order was: "Exterminate every living thing so that the land might be purified." The sad thing is that today similar terrors and murders are being carried out, again in the name of God and religion.

Sunday, November 20

The other day Letitia and I went to the hospital to see a woman who epitomizes human tragedy. Eleven years ago she was diagnosed as having terminal cancer. After a long series of painful and debilitating radiation and chemotherapy treatments, she emerged with the cancer in remission.

Soon after this she contracted a form of herpes along with a staph infection. Because of this deep scars formed across her forehead and she became blind in one eye. She told us that this disfigurement caused her husband to leave her. Thus the burden of raising three small children fell squarely on her shoulders. The pressure got so great that she eventually suffered a nervous breakdown. And, as if that weren't enough, right after she recovered from the breakdown the cancer became active again.

As we talked, she said that she had no fear of death, but she did fear the process of dying especially since the doctors said that the cancer had spread to her lungs. This terrified her for she could envision herself choking to death.

What a sad figure. What a tragic situation. What a horrible past. So another tragedy occurs which the world will never hear about. How many people right now are in similar or even worse straits?

While I was holding her hand and listening to her story, an elderly woman in the next bed began to sob uncontrollably. The three people standing around her tried to console her, but they could not. They all looked so helpless. This was the cancer ward, so she too was probably suffering from the dreaded disease.

During our conversation, the woman we were with referred to her own mental state as "black despair." Such despair registered in her eyes and on her countenance. But then somewhat later I saw her eyes begin to soften and some of the lines of hopelessness fade from her face. Perhaps she had momentarily forgotten about her plight. Perhaps she was feeling some of the love which we were directing to her. Whatever it was, I saw a release, a relaxing, a sense of ease within her. As we got up to leave she reached out and grasped our hands. She pulled us gently down to her and hugged us. We kissed her on the cheek. We felt for this moment a deep kinship and a love, this woman and us, this woman we'd met only an hour ago. And we were grateful. And now she looked peaceful.

Will our meeting and the love change her feelings about her predicament? Will she now feel more like living than dying? Will she be healed? I don't know. Truly, only God knows, but if she desires God's healing energy with all her heart I know she can be healed.

We will diligently attempt to help her in the ways that we can. We will be in contact with her. We will direct the love we feel from Spirit to her. This is what we can do. But the real healing, if it's to come, must come from her desire to live and her desire to feel Spirit's love loving her.

I recall some of my more difficult times in dealing with the cancer. Sometimes I could feel a lot of Spirit and still not feel the tumors being touched. Then I began to realize that Spirit wasn't touching the tumors because there was tension, tightness—a holding on to those areas where the tumors were. So I began consciously to release those areas and as I did the love would flow into and fill all those places which needed the healing.

There was often an extreme resistance to releasing and yielding the body. It was as if those places of disease were wound up so tightly that they refused to let go. So it took a dedicated persistence to get the resistance to diminish. And then the miracle of Spirit dissolving the tumors would take place.

If when we're sick or in pain we can begin to yield all those places of the body which hurt to Spirit's energy, then a process begins which I would call the subtilization of the senses. With this process the body—which before felt so opaque, so hard and impenetrable—now begins through the energy to feel more transparent and less material. Through such a change in our feeling-base, the sickness or pain, so paramount just moments ago, begins to float away. It must. For these sensations can only maintain themselves within the intensity and density of the senses. These sensations cannot exist when one feels the energy of Spirit in the places where the problem is.

According to medical science, when a cancerous tumor is being formed, a protective wall is built around it by the bad cells, and this effectively shuts out the good cells from destroying the bad. Does this happen because of the many fears we have about an enemy like cancer invading our body? If so then it's imperative that we release the fear and release those areas where we feel the tumors so that the energy of Spirit can heal us.

Dr. Carl Simonton* has said that cancer should dissipate as readily as the common cold. And it would,

---

*A noted radiologist who uses mental imagery along with radiation therapy to treat cancer.

I'm sure, if it didn't have such horrible images attached to it. I believe the images which create the fearful thoughts *are* what keeps cancer alive within the body. This has been my experience in dealing with cancer.

Wednesday, November 23

Today while waiting to visit a person in the hospital, I struck up a conversation with a man who was probably in his early sixties. He told me that he had lived in an industrial town in Ohio all his life. Our talk was cordial until I mentioned that I lived in California and enjoyed it very much. He then began to chide me for living in a state filled with a bunch of eccentrics, Communists and hippies. When I objected and tried to explain that most Californians are average, normal people, he rejected this and became even more belligerent.

After a while I stopped defending and began listening. Having no one to debate with, he soon simmered down. Finally we stopped talking. After a space he said, "You know, about thirty years ago I had an opportunity to move to California. I was offered a real good job out there, but I didn't take it because I didn't want to give up what I had in Ohio—you know, job security, children, friends, relatives. Well, I made a mistake. I should have gone 'cause my wife's dead, my parents are both gone, and my kids live a long way away, so I hardly ever see them. Oh, I still have my same job. That hasn't changed. But God, I know now that I should have taken the chance and gone to California."

"Do you think that would have changed your life for the better?" I asked.

"Oh I don't know" he sighed. "Maybe not. But I wish I had taken the chance. Then, at least, I would have found out."

Change promises unfamiliarity, insecurity, and a possible foundering in life. With change we may still find ourselves unhappy. But unless we make changes when we have the light to see that a change is necessary our lives can become set. In this there can be many regrets.

Thursday, November 24

You begin the steady climb up toward the waterfall several miles away. At first you feel the muscles of the legs pushing your body up the steps. Then you begin to let go of the legs and all the body. Your attempt is to have the power of the energy propel you up those steps. So you need to feel the energy in the legs. And you realize that to feel the energy there you must let go of the muscles so that they are actually flaccid, so that they are not the worker in the pushing.

After a while you begin to feel the release and the in-filling of the energy. Now the energy is building upon itself. Before long you can feel yourself being powered up the steps by the energy. The walking is now effortless. There's no more sense of being weary, even though you've been walking steadily for half an hour. You stop and sit down to have lunch with your son and wife. All the while that you're eating, you keep released to the energy, for you know there's at least another hour's walk ahead.

This time the climb takes you through a heavy mist which dampens your clothes and hair and makes the steps that you're climbing slippery. Going up there's little danger of falling. Coming down might be another matter, for there's no railing to hold on to and the drop off to your left is critically steep and very deep.

With each step you feel stronger, for now the energy

is in full control. There's absolutely no effort in walking. Finally, almost before you realize it, you're at the top. The view is magnificent. The water from the huge fall cascades down the rocks and plunges into the canyon hundreds of feet below. You note that there's another waterfall even higher, so you all begin to climb toward that. Within a half-hour or so you're at the foot of the falls watching torrents of water rolling and splashing down the mountain. You all sit down and watch. Your son goes to the edge of the falls and throws a rock down into the bottom of the canyon. It seems to take forever to hit.

All told you climbed for two and a half hours. One would think that there'd be sore muscles and weariness to deal with later, for there is also the walk down the steps. And although you do some hiking you're not at all used to hiking this size mountain. But as you find out that evening and the next morning there's no extra weariness to deal with, nor are there any sore muscles. Can you say that the muscles weren't being used? If you had reached down and touched the legs while you were walking, you certainly would have felt the firmness in the legs, but was the firmness caused by the energy or by the muscles? Since the muscles weren't at all sore or tired, you surmise that the energy was the real motive power for the walking up that mountain.

Sunday, November 27

This morning I walked in the gray dawn and sat on a rock near the sand. I felt again that great sense of emptiness which is really a great fullness of the energy. It was emptiness because there was no sense of body, there was no thought. I realized that thought was totally gone because it had no bodily sensations to react to.

So instead of feeling myself as a body and mind, I felt this beautiful sense of space, of emptiness. And as I looked around I saw everything—the houses, the trees, the ocean, the gulls, the people far up the beach—as living in that emptiness. It was as if the emptiness surrounded, enveloped everything. Things seemed as if they were on a stage supported and upheld by this loving emptiness.

I could have sat on that rock all day and been totally contented, for there was nothing pressing in mind or body to move me off the rock; I felt no impulse or intention or motivation that would get me to move. There was only love communicating with Love.

This morning's experience makes me realize that a primary ingredient needed to feel Spirit is the emptiness of self, for as long as I'm full with my problems, with my thoughts, with my feelings, with my hopes, with my desires then Spirit will naturally be excluded.

The releasing of the body seems to empty the accumulations of self, for the body, it appears, is the reservoir of self—the accumulator of past griefs, hopes, fears, pleasure. And from this reservoir of the past I act, I think, I hope, I desire; I live what I call my human life. The body in conjunction with the mind *is* the self. So with the release or stilling of either the body or mind, then the self is at least partially emptied.

So much attention in meditation is focused on the mind. But it's important to look at the body also. If one experiments one finds that it's much easier to release the body, and consequently to still the body, than it is to still the mind. I feel that if the mind is somewhat quiet and the body released, then Spirit will naturally be there for anyone and everyone to experience, for it's always there when one is not.

This evening we drove by my former home, the home which, prior to meeting Letitia, I lived in alone for eight years. How much I learned there about life. How much I learned about solitude, both its joys and its hardships. Solitude is not for everyone. It's difficult, at times, even for those who are deeply attuned to its quiet pace and peaceful setting. But if there were hard times, there were more often times of pure joy, of communion and of love.

I remember years ago when I first drove into Cambria wondering if this was the place for me to live. I was immediately struck by the quaintness and sleepiness of the town. Main Street was lined with old brick and wooden buildings, and the residential streets surrounding the center of town were dotted with old wooden houses dating from the nineteenth century.

When I went into the real estate office, the secretary told me quite positively that there just wasn't anything to rent. But, she added, if I wanted I could check with her boss when he got back.

I remember I drove across the main highway and into the pine-covered hills. The day was glistening, bright and beautiful. Several times I stopped the car, got out, and just listened to the sounds and looked at the sights—the birds, the isolated roads, the tall grass bending in the breeze. There was peace and silence and a sense of sacredness everywhere.

Rounding a bend in the road, I saw off to my right an A-frame house. It was nestled in the trees and had beamed ceilings and floor-to-roof picture windows which looked out toward the ocean. What a joy it would be to live there, I thought. I could picture myself sitting on the front deck writing, or just enjoying the view and the solitude. The house was perfect. And the beautiful thing

was that there wasn't another house around. I'd be totally alone. Then my daydream suddenly shattered, for
standing at the window peering out at me was a stern-
faced woman.

When I got back to the real estate office, the broker
told me there was nothing available anywhere around
and nothing was likely to become available. Cambria
just didn't have many rentals, he said. And those who
did rent stayed for years.

I remember how let down I felt. I almost knew that
this was the place for me, and yet it seemed the door
had shut tightly. Then as I was leaving, just as though it
had been planned, the secretary announced that some
people renting from the realtor had called and said that
because of the husband's illness they had to move back
to the city. The broker pondered for several moments.
Then grumbling something about how he knew I
wouldn't like the place because it was so isolated, he
told me to come with him.

We drove across the highway and up and down some
hilly dirt roads. As we rounded a bend I saw the house I
had liked so much off to the right. Then before I knew it
we were driving up the driveway! I just couldn't believe
it! I was ecstatic!

This beautiful home was the home I lived in, wrote in,
and loved in. How much I learned living alone. How
much I have learned and am learning while living with
Letitia, my beautiful wife.

Tuesday, November 29

Often when someone first feels the energy, it sets up a
remembering—a remembering that sometime before, in
some place, one has felt this energy, for most of us,
perhaps all of us, have felt the energy of Spirit. But we

have forgotten the feeling because other feelings—material feelings—have captured our lives. Or perhaps we have forgotten because we thought it just happened and would never happen again. Or perhaps we have forgotten because we didn't realize that the energy comes from a Source—a Source which is real, aware, intelligent, and caring, a Source we may someday call God.

Wednesday, November 30

The near-death experiencer reports that the universe is not crazy and chaotic but intelligent and purposeful. What I see in these reports is that through the loss of one's material sensing of life, which occurs when one is near death, *then* the universe appears purposeful and intelligent. This is similar to the experience one has when one feels a depth of Spirit. During these episodes, one oftentimes experiences, sees, the universe much more translucently. Thus the hard realities of matter—the deaths, accidents, sickness, terror—lose much of their impact. And without these negatives the universe is purposeful; the universe is really a beautiful place to be and to live in.

Wednesday, December 7

Saroyan* once said, "All comedians are people who deeply consider the human experience not only a dirty trick perpetrated by a totally meaningless series of accidents, but an unbearable ordeal every day, which can be made tolerable only by mockery in one form or another. They like to see you feeling amused enough to

---

*American novelist and playwrite.

92

forget, that you really feel terrible about the whole thing outraged at the first because you have been born and then outraged because you must die."

A succinct analysis of the material condition of life. Not at all applicable to the condition of a life lived with Spirit.

Thursday, December 8

I remember the many hospitals we visited while distributing the *Kingdom of God*.* To see so much misery housed under one roof truly reveals the human condition, and this in the land of plenty, in the land where medical help is most abundant. To see these things makes you think deeply about life. It makes you awaken to the fact that material life is so miserable for so many people. It makes you want to reach out and help them.

Saturday, December 10

Krishnamurti maintains that if we could just see the source of our misery and conflict—which is the me in all its actions—and put an end to this me, then we could live happily on this beautiful earth.

Even though putting an end to the me, the ego, is a huge step in solving our problems, I don't think it's the total solution. The total solution is, I believe, to realize that we live within the confines of matter. Until that prison of materiality is broken open, we will never be ultimately happy or free.

---

*John's first book. (Marina Del Rey, Calif: Devorss & Co.) John and Letitia presented copies of the book to numerous hospitals throughout the west.

Breaking open the prison doors, this is what the energy can do.

Of course if there is no me, then there's no entity to realize that he's confined in matter. My point is that this me-less-ness for most of us is temporary—we must earn a living, talk to people, take action, all of which requires thought, and this creates the ego. Therefore, we all come back to the realization that matter imprisons us, although one less entrenched in the me is less bound by this imprisonment.

Friday, December 11

Been feeding two jays for several months. When they see us they come swooping down from the trees for a peanut. Knowing that we always have a fresh supply at hand, they'll sit patiently on the fence until we fetch one for them. The male insists that he gets his first. And if the female dares to try to grab the first peanut for herself, the male will chase her off.

What a delight it is to feel their soft feet on my hand. Oftentimes one of them will decide to stay there for a while. Then we'll have a talk. I'll tell it how much I love them and enjoy their coming around each day. It will respond, usually with a gurgling in the throat. These small gems of nature with their shrill whistles and happy manner bring an extra delight to the day.

Many times they'll come join us for breakfast in the courtyard. Sometimes they'll just squat on our knees with their legs pulled up under them and their feathers fluffed out, looking totally contented. At these times I know that they're picking up on the energy, because wild birds just don't act this way. How soft their eyes and bodies become as we tell them how beautiful they are and how much we care for them. The creatures of nature and man aren't that much different. All of us want to feel that we're appreciated and loved.

Wednesday, December 14

One of Einstein's greatest quests was to prove that the universe's material forces are unified, interrelated and have some principle or law behind their operation. He never found such proof. In fact I read just recently that today's scientists question whether matter operates according to any immutable law or principle.

I also question whether it does, for when you feel and see matter's world and then you switch and feel and see the world of Spirit, you find a vast difference. Whereas the world of matter consists of a hodgepodge of disparate, unconnected, isolated objects each operating from imperfect physical forces, Spirit's world, needing no objects to fulfill itself, is one and operates from a power which is perfect.

On a walk this afternoon I saw a Monarch butterfly fluttering on the ground, seemingly suffering death-throes. As I got closer I saw a bee was stinging it. Chasing the bee away, I began sending the energy to this beautiful little life. I also spoke to it and said that it would be all right for it was really living in the energy of God's kingdom. As I was working I had looked away. When I looked back I saw the little creature flying for the sky.

Friday, December 16

When I feel the energy deeply, I realize that my true being is a part of Spirit, the energy's source. The relationship is that of Spirit governing and giving life to my being. Without Spirit I would have no being-life. This life-giving Source, Spirit, exists in a realm entirely different from this sphere of matter and material existence.

Conversely, when I feel life more physically, materially, I realize that my human life is controlled by the mind. Without the mind I would have no human life. This life-giving material source, the mind, exists in a realm of matter which is a realm entirely different from and opposite to Spirit's life.

Perceiving these parallels between Spirit's life and material life, I ask whether matter's duplication of Spirit's life was accidental or intentional. Whatever the truth is, if one is devoted to living a life with Spirit, it's important to realize and absolutely essential to *feel* that one's eternal being is of Spirit and with Spirit. Then when the mind and bodily senses utter their cries that one is sick, depressed, frustrated, fearful, stressed, one can negate this uneternal falsehood and yield this false sense of life to the real sense of life—Spirit's eternal life.

It was great fun, while writing *The Sojourner* (John began writing this unpublished book in 1970) to sit down at the typewriter and ask questions about life, questions for which I had absolutely no answer. Why time and what about eternity? Is there a God who really cares for us? Is there life after death? The answers—if indeed they were answers in the sense of being a final solution—would come in the language of the earth, in words and phrases whose essence and fiber were a part of nature.

In the Sojourner's world life was much simpler—not necessarily easier but simpler. This was because he lived so long ago. And the Sojourner, who was really myself, was attempting to live life simply; he was attempting to live life without the complexity of being told what to think, what to do, what to believe, what to be. Therefore, he had to question everything; he had to deal with life's problems with a sense of immediacy, a sense of freshness, a sense of not knowing what life's answers were. Thus he lived a vital life—a life where he was constantly challenged, was constantly discovering, was constantly learning. This is the life I envisioned then. This is the life I try to live today.

Wednesday, December 21

Just reread *The Kingdom of God*. This little book helps me so much to release deeply to Spirit, for the book was written from that position. It was written when I was so sick with the cancer that I had to keep releasing my body, keep releasing my whole being to the energy or I just wouldn't have made it.

I remember the day the book was "given." I was at a deep and frustrating time with my writing. I didn't know where to turn; I didn't know whether to quit and do something else or what. Then one morning as I was coming down the stairs from the bedroom, suddenly and right out of the blue came the words, "You're going to explain me differently." There wasn't a doubt who the "me" was referring to. It referred to Jesus. I'd recently been poring over his words in an attempt to find out how he healed so that I could help heal myself.

On that day I was given a direction and on that day I began outlining the book I knew I was to write. I was helped immensely with the book's writing. I was given insights and understanding which I didn't know were there.

The interesting thing about the words "explain me differently" is that the book turned out this way. I think I did explain Jesus differently. It may not have been the way he would have explained himself at the time, since he had been brought up in the Jewish faith and with a Messianic tradition. I think, though, today he might look at himself differently, having the benefit of science, communication, and the history of civilization to view things from.

Thursday, December 22

Been reading a biography of Leonardo da Vinci. I find what he once wrote about solitude interesting. He said, "If you are alone you belong entirely to yourself. If you are accompanied by even one companion you belong only half to yourself, or even less, in proportion to the thoughtlessness of his conduct; and if you have more than one companion you will fall more deeply into the same plight."

He states exactly, I feel, why so many creative, sensitive and artistic people seek long periods of solitude. It isn't for the most part that these people are inclined to be solitaries. It's that banal companionship can dissipate one's creative energy. I love being with people who are interested in life and interested in discovering what life is about. If I can't be with such people, then I'd prefer to spend time alone to write, to read, to be, and to discover with and be close to Spirit.

Saturday, December 24

Christmas Eve and we're at Pine Mountain (a small community in Southern California's Los Padres Mountains). There's only a touch of snow on the mountains since we're having a dry and warm winter.

Christmas is probably the most kindly of all times of year. We turn from our harried, hurried lives, and for the first time perhaps in a long while, we begin to see life with calm and loving eyes. We're in the mood to give more than receive, to be generous rather than covetous, to love and care instead of being centered so much on self. One can feel these changes in the atmosphere at Christmas. It truly is a blessed time for most. But surely it's a sorrowful time for others who for a multitude of reasons don't have their friends and families with them. For Letitia and me this Christmas Eve is certainly blessed with a fullness of Spirit. And we are deeply grateful.

Sunday, December 25

Christmas morning and I'll be alone today. (Letitia had to be in Los Angeles.) And yet I'm not alone. I sense Spirit's energy with me. I feel Spirit's caring and closeness. I'm so blessed.

Shanna (John's daughter), God bless her, called first thing this morning. What a beautiful soul she is. She's a flower in the wilderness of the world. I pray that she learns what it means to live deeply with love. It's the only way to live greatly, fully. It's really not only the ultimate meaning of life, it's the only meaning.

Shanna and I talked about her childhood days and some of the times we spent in Ojai on her birthday. What a delight it was to ride bikes, swim, play miniature golf, eat at restaurants and discuss the "deeper" issues of life. I remember one time as we were driving to Ojai—she was about seven—when she turned to me and said, "You know, daddy, I think it's about time that you and I had a serious discussion about some things." She was serious. And, yes, we did have some serious discussions about several things. It was amazing how clear and unencumbered her young mind was.

Those times of innocence I especially enjoyed. I enjoyed participating with her and David and all my children during these years of their youth, for there was a different quality of love, a quality that can never quite be recaptured. And that's O.K., for everyone must grow up someday. But hopefully grownups will keep the innocence they once had, even though they must deal with life's larger issues. Thankfully, all my children have.

So what shall I do on this beautiful bright Christmas day? It really doesn't matter. Whatever I do will be joy because the energy is full. Later perhaps I'll take a long walk on the ranch. I love to go down the mountain toward the ocean and get lost in the woods. I find so much magic there: the magic of watching and listening to the birds, of watching and listening to the wind coursing through the trees, of watching and listening to the

water from the creeks splashing down the mountain-
sides. And perhaps today I'll see something different like
a bobcat or a fox. I've never seen a fox around here but
I know there are some. Maybe today.

Tuesday, December 27

Spirit is a whole new life; it's a whole new energy
field. Spirit's life is in the now, in the eternal, therefore
it views life eternally. Spirit doesn't need to deal with
time as we do to remember, to cogitate, to live in the
past, for there's no past with Spirit. Spirit's life is totally
different from our life of the mind and senses which is
bound to time, bound to the past.

Thursday, December 29

On letting go of self, we'll oftentimes feel ourselves
changing from one energy base to the other—from matter's energy and feeling to Spirit's. Now we're in a new
state of life, of being. We find we can look about and
see the same trees, birds, mountains, and people that we
have always seen, but all our feelings about these things
have changed. We now feel at-one with everything.
We're communing with everything. We feel love for
everything. Surely the world we're seeing now is the
world which God has made.

We intuit, almost know, that we're living and feeling
the same energy of life and of perfection which God,
Spirit feels. And from this place of perfection we realize
that somehow, in some way, a cloak of materiality has
been thrown over the world. Because of the cloak, we
who live here suffer, struggle, and die, or so we assume,
for when the cloak has been removed—if only for a little

while—we find that real life is not that way at all. Real life is filled with beauty, joy, harmony. There is nothing else.

A woman recently said to me, "It would be wonderful to feel the energy all the time because all your problems in life would be solved." This, of course, isn't the case, for though a number of us feel the energy constantly, there's still the problem of what to do with the other sense of life—the material sense—with all its thoughts and feelings.

Today I feel Spirit deeply. Therefore I can drop every arising of a negative thought or sensation and let the energy of Spirit absorb the negative and remove it. This is a marvelous place to be. But it's not always this easy. That's where devotion and desire come in, for when the problems get tough, and they certainly do at times, then one needs to have enough desire for Spirit to stick with Spirit and work the problem through no matter how long or how many obstacles are encountered.

Caroline, Letitia, and I have often discussed what it is that gives some people a deep devotion to Spirit while other people have hardly any. The answer we have found so far is that somewhere along the way Spirit has to implant the devotion, which is really a love for Spirit. Spirit implants this devotion through our feeling Spirit's life. Without our first feeling Spirit, we can't have devotion, for we don't know what Spirit is.

Friday, December 30

Linda (John's older daughter) came visiting for a couple of days. Linda doesn't try to be funny, she just naturally is. When I'm around her I see life from a humorous point of view. She may be telling a serious story about one of her "tragic" life situations or relating something serious that's happened to one of her friends. All of a sudden right in the middle of the story she'll say something ridiculously funny without even meaning to. And we'll all burst out laughing.

Last night she was relating a story of a friend who is going through a divorce. The story really was sad, and we all felt the sadness, but the way Linda was relating it was getting to be funny. Somewhere along the way she made one of her unintentional double-entendres, and we all began to howl.

What a gift laughter can be when it comes from that wellspring of freedom and joy.

I'm reminded of what Saroyan said about comedians using humor to ameliorate their inner agony. Linda, as far as I know, hasn't suffered much agony, but she surely has faced more trying situations than the other children. So maybe her naturally humorous way of viewing life is her way of compensating for some of her pain.

Besides humor, she also has a good heart and a spiritual side. I'm so thankful that all the children have felt Spirit. If none of them ever go for Spirit like I have, that's O.K. They at least know that it's there to heal and to help with all their life problems. Mainly, it's there to give them a sense of peace and joy.

Sunday, January 1, 1984

Albert Camus* once told about a time he took a solitary stroll in France along a street by the side of the sea. As he walked along he suddenly lost himself; for a

*French novelist and dramatist.

while memory, thought, normal human reactions were suspended. What resulted was that everything he saw—the people, the flowers, the trees, the sea—he saw with a dispassionate love. He was removed from the world and yet he felt love for the world. He tells of sitting down at a sidewalk cafe and feeling absolute wonder at the beauty and simplicity of life. He was literally living in heaven, he said, and never wanted the experience to end.

But it did end. And from that day on the experience must have haunted him, for he knew he had experienced *life*, and to return to nonlife—the ordinary, mundane way we usually view and experience things—could never be entirely acceptable. Perhaps this is a reason for the stoical cynicism which flows through his books.

In Camus' *The Stranger* the protagonist constantly declares that nothing really matters; pain is as good as pleasure and death is as good as life. That's why when he's accused of a capital offense he puts up only a perfunctory effort to save his life.

Viewed from Spirit's energy, nothing in this material world really matters absolutely. All is of little value save the love we feel for others, the compassion we feel, the help we give to others. All of one's self-centered interests and actions are for naught, really, and will disappear and soon be forgotten. What will not be forgotten are those acts which emanate from love.

Monday, January 2

I find in an Ionesco* journal I'm reading many Camus-like experiences. During one of them, Ionesco says, "Nothing is true outside of this." The puzzling thing to me is, if these revelatory experiences are the only truth, then why didn't he pursue this truth? (Perhaps he has more than I know.)

Most of us, though, even after experiences such as these, don't pursue them to find if they can be repeated or even lived with. Is it because we think the experience is so unnatural that we could never have it again? It is unnatural for our egos and the life we live in matter. But for our beings these experiences are completely natural; for our beings, I feel beyond all doubt, are connected to that other realm and part of it.

Wednesday, January 4

I've been influenced by hundreds of people throughout my life—parents, teachers, friends, ministers, writers, musicians, psychologists, scientists, and so many others. I think it's imperative that I learn from others if I'm to grow and to understand. If it hadn't been for these many people, my learning about the human condition would

---

*Eugene Ionesco, French dramatist.

have been dwarfed. Nor, perhaps, would I have realized that there was a real God to be found in a world where belief, faith, and dogma are the religious substitutes for experiencing Reality.

On the other hand, there are many times when I need to be free of all past influences, for they can keep me from discovering anew for myself. This morning was just such a time. I had been walking for a while through a broad, solitary meadow surrounded by mountains. Coming upon a fallen tree by the edge of the meadow, I sat down. The day was magical. All of nature's life was lilting and rejoicing in soft warm breezes and full bright sunlight. Overhead was the clearest blue sky I have ever seen.

As I sat there feeling a fullness of the energy within and without, I began to listen to the sounds all about. The scraping of a chameleon's feet on a log, the bright whistle of a flicker, the rustling of the leaves all served as a symphony of sound which was part of the energy I was feeling. And it occurred to me that right then someone else's thoughts, someone else's experiences, someone else's ideas, no matter how lofty, would only be an interference, a distraction to the reality of this moment. Love for me this morning was a new discovery even though I'd felt the same love many times before.

And this is the marvelous thing about the energy of love: It's always refreshingly new and joyous no matter how many times you experience it. It's new because there's nothing within the energy that's old; the energy is always now, in the present and eternal. And it's joyous because there's not one particle of unhappiness, sorrow, grief, or despair within it.

Friday, January 6

While driving along a highway with lush green moun-

106

tains on one side and the wind-whipped ocean on the other, you suddenly realize that you're looking at everything with old eyes—with eyes which have seen these things dozens of times before. And you realize that there's no reason to see through the eyes of the past. You can see with new eyes. All it entails is to drop the past. And you do. In an instant all the memories of how those mountains and the ocean once looked are gone. And you find yourself immediately in a different dimension where all is new and joyously love-filled. This dimension is a self-contained world of perfection, love, and total bliss. There's nothing within this dimension that can make it otherwise; there's no animosity, anxiety, or conflict of any kind. All is total harmony.

You drive along marveling that you can be in touch with such a world so full of life, newness, and love. You want to pray and thank God, but you don't because you don't want to have even a prayer interrupt this livingness that's happening right now. You drive on feeling this life pulsating in you and all about. Are you seeing the mountains and ocean with new eyes? It's no longer a question. The love is all now that matters. And that is all-encompassing. Your total involvement is with that.

You look about and see everything, but you react to nothing. You look at the mountains and see them, but since you're not reacting to them there's no verbalizing about them. You don't say they're beautiful or make any judgment about anything, for you're far away from that judgmental world. And since the world you're now participating in is full of perfection, it is beyond all judging. You do realize that the whole world is incredibly beautiful but you don't let this evaluation pull you back into the world, and it will if you begin thinking. Thinking is from here. Over there there's no need to think. What need is there to think when all is right.

You stop the car and walk down to a solitary beach. You sit down on a rock and watch the gulls working against the wind and some shore birds searching for food. The intensity of the love has diminished somewhat. The high winds seem to have drawn you back into the world of feeling and thus into thought.

On the drive back home the intensity begins to increase again. You're away from the distraction of the wind and being cold. Now you look at the mountains and ocean. You ask if these things are being seen anew. And they are. But just such a question, you find, is pulling you back into the world. So you drop the question and enter more deeply into the love.

You get back home and sit down to write about the experience. You're writing now from the experience, not about it. And yet words are needed, which is verbal evaluation. Words are evaluation. Words to a great extent are what keep us locked in the world of the mind and senses, keep us locked in the world of the old with its memories and evaluations. But the words you write now are coming from that other place, so you're not caught in the world of evaluating. Thus the experiencing is still there. And you realize that it will be with you all day, so long as you keep self out of the way. Even if self gets in the way for a while you know you will be able to drop it. And as you do that other life will be there.

Saturday, January 7

The young couple who visited us last night expressed dissatisfaction with themselves and their lives. They said that they felt useless and unproductive, not really using their God-given capacities; they felt afraid about their futures, especially if they maintained their patterns; they felt unloved, for those closest to them were critical of their behavior; they felt trapped by their behavior because they didn't know how to break it. All of this caused them to be confused, to race about, never to settle down so that they could look at themselves as they were and not as they'd like to be.

We discussed how important it was to see ourselves honestly and objectively, for such objectivity calms the self and allows for clarity. In this clarity there comes a natural transcendence over our problems, for there's a glimpse of our real timeless identity with Spirit.

To understand the problem of human life was their greatest challenge. They saw this, at least for a while and hopefully longer. The core of everyone's problem is this self which constantly hounds us with its thoughts, with its desires, with its conflicts, with its agitations and anxieties. And even when many of us see this, we don't know what to do about it; our confusion is understandable.

When we come to that point of realization where we can clearly see that this human self is the main problem of our life because it creates all conflict, then we're at the place of action. The kind of action we take will vary according to where we are psychologically, intellectually, spiritually, and according to what we feel we're most attuned with. Thus some of us will turn to psychology, New Age methods, religion, etc.

There will be others who will be inclined to ask themselves if there really is a Truth, a Reality, a God beyond all of the mind's thoughts, beyond all the mind's hopes, projections, and imaginings. For these people the answer can only be found in a truth they can feel, in a truth they can experience, in a truth that they can honestly say is real to them. For these people, the solution to the problem of the self is to find that truth or reality, to know it, to feel it, for they intuit that when they do they will have found the ultimate solution to the problem of life.

We decided to get lost for a few days. So we drove inland searching for some place where we'd never been before. By lunch time we found the spot. The town was old. Many of the buildings had cornerstones dating back to the last century.

After lunch we wandered about gazing into store windows and looking at the flowers, the people, the birds, and everything else there was to see. After a while we came across an old wooden one-room structure—the town library. We went inside and began browsing through the books. Almost immediately I caught sight of one by Herman Hesse, *Wandering*. For years I've enjoyed his books.

The inside cover said that it was the last book he'd written before his death. Thumbing slowly through the pages, I was immediately struck by the feeling and thought behind his words. I sat down and for the next several hours I read those 109 pages, carefully savoring the book's flavor. Hesse obviously had taken great pains in writing the book and I was going to take care in reading it.

What a lift I received from that little book. To find a kinship with someone is one of the most beautiful experiences. As we walked to the car, I felt a warmth and an increased appreciation for life and a gratitude that there have been and are today loving, sensitive people. I give thanks to Hesse for giving the world this beautiful book.

Saturday, January 14

The energy of love has no relationship to thinking.

When the energy is deep there is no thinking. There may be considering, but not thinking. Considering is a gentle, leisurely, more transparent contemplation of things. With considering, thoughts pass through one without attaching to one's self. In this way one can deeply contemplate an issue or a problem and still keep at a proper distance from it so that an intelligent solution can present itself. With considering, love rather than thought dominates.

When the energy is felt, one can do the million and one things the human being does and do them with joy, with freedom, with delight, because the emphasis is not on the me. With love the me has diminished or is extinguished, thus in the place of self one feels a rich, full sense of being.

It's difficult to feel the energy of love, at times, because the lion of thought in conjunction with the human senses want to dominate, want to rule, want to control one's life. And when it does, love is gone. Thinking is insidious, for even when there's love, thinking may step in and halt the love affair.

Thought is always thinking of itself. It can do nothing else. It can perform no other service. Thought's hue and cry is, "What's in it for me?" Thought is the epitome of self-focus and self-concern. The more one thinks the more self-centered one becomes. Thought weaves a web of restriction about us and, seeing no way out, we live in this restriction.

Love, on the contrary, brings one into freedom. Love *is* freedom and flourishes in freedom. Love is the breaking through of the miasma of the mind and senses and emerging into a universe where Spirit abides.

Thought and love. Which will win out? This is a major challenge, perhaps the greatest challenge of all.

When one becomes aware of thought, actually sees the moving of thought as one would see an object move, then thought slows down and eventually stops. And

with thought's stoppage there's a loss of recognition of self—I have lost my history and now am living and being without a sense of ego, of image. Now I am pure being and living with the energy.

The awareness with the energy is entirely different from human awareness. With the energy one's awareness is broad, expansive, not limited to the things which one's mind is attracted to. Thus there's space and freedom in this awareness. Also there's the awareness of an endless depth of life which thought can never be aware of. The awareness of the depth is endless because there is no boundary of thought to limit the awareness.

This evening while sitting before the fire—Letitia was outside watching the sunset on the deck—I watched the movement of my thought. I wasn't so interested in watching what I was thinking about but in the movement of thought. At first it was quite a fast movement and difficult to follow. But after a while the movement began to slow down. Finally it came to a stop. And at that instant there appeared to be a flash of light which seemed to go right through my head. It felt cleansing. It felt enlightening and clarifying. It felt entirely good. Was it from Spirit? I don't know, for the feeling of love didn't accompany the flash. But who knows for sure what Spirit brings and how it is brought?

People who meditate—also many of us who feel Spirit—spend so much time trying to quiet thought, stop thought, quell thought, when it's really not essential. If we just simply examine our thought while we are thinking, then thought stops. This is because thought occurs in unawareness, not in awareness. When we become aware of thought for the simple purpose of examining it—not trying to stop it—then it ends. It's all so simple and requires no effort.

Monday, January 16

Beethoven, often accused of impiety, wrote on the first page of his "Credo" (a section of the *Missa Solem-*

113

nis), "God above all. . .God has never deserted me." He felt this despite the fact that he, perhaps the greatest of all composers, suffered the worst of all afflictions for a musician—deafness.

How much I relate to Beethoven's words! As I was suffering from what the world calls cancer and from what I believed to be cancer, and while going through "the tortures of the damned," I seldom had long periods when Spirit wasn't with me. Otherwise, I most likely wouldn't be here.

Tuesday, January 17

The persons who suffer the most pain often have the potential to go the highest with Spirit, for pain drives one away from disharmonious matter and into the harmony of Spirit.

Wednesday, January 18

The ocean was spectacular this morning! The sunlight flashing off the kelp on the beach, the shore birds flitting here and there and flying off as I came near, the beads of white froth splashing off the sand as the waves hit, all these sights and sounds I was seeing and hearing in an eternal way—in a way of freedom and contentment. It was as if everything was right, everything was in place, everything was bathed in perfection. It wasn't that matter life, nature life, human life were perfect, but that I was seeing from the eyes of perfection; I was seeing with the eyes of Spirit.

Such seeing isn't imagining. It's real and more substantial than matter's way of seeing, than matter's way of life. What gives Spirit's way of seeing and Spirit's life substantiality is the energy of Spirit. Spirit is an energy, a life, a substantialness that one can feel all through one's being.

Friday, January 20

As I drove up a road bordered by a creek this morning, the energy of love was again there. The energy was a special blessing this day for I felt tired and worn out and really not naturally close to Spirit. My mind seemed to be listless and lifeless, just like my body. When the energy came it took over these places of the body and mind, and because it was so strong, it stunned the body and mind and made them silent and sensationless. It would have taken more effort to think and to feel than to just go with the energy. And go with it I did. It was beautiful. It was joy. It was an everlasting life I was part of. In the midst of the joy I realized that at this moment I had everything; everything had been given me and I desired absolutely nothing. How could I desire more than this joy, this love? It's only when the energy diminishes that one thinks again in terms of wanting more. But now everything was perfection. Everything was bliss.

Saturday, January 21

Caroline (co-author of *Conversations in Spirit*), after she had felt the energy for a while, began referring to it as God. Since I seldom used this word, I asked her why she did. She replied that it was because the energy was the truth of her being. And since it was, then this truth had to be God.

God is an odd word. Religions for centuries have seemed to own it. In my earlier days, I accepted what the minister, the priest, the guru, the master said about God—I accepted their definition and understanding of God rather than seeking out God for myself. I did so because I thought they knew. After all weren't they the experts, the ones who had devoted all their lives to knowing God?

What the word *God* describes for me now is a sense of energy or life which I feel. The essence of this sense is love. I call it love because it's such an incredibly beautiful sense of purity, perfection, freedom, and joy. What more can God be than this love? Surely the joy and love I feel now is greater than all the gods I once accepted or read about, learned about or heard about.

For so long the word God related to the Christian concepts I'd learned as a child. I can't recall ever believing that Jesus was God, even though I was warned constantly by several ministers that I might suffer in Hell for my disbelief.

Despite their warnings, I just couldn't accept their concepts about God, for I felt something very different; I felt a sense of excitement about living, a sense that life could be a marvelous adventure, a sense that I and everyone could live in freedom and be rejoiceful.

Even today I often hesitate to use the word *God* save when I'm conversing with someone I can meet on a common ground of experience. Then the word can be rich and meaningful. It can be the recognition between people of the magnificent purity, of the true sacredness of that life of absolute love to which the name *God* refers.

At the far end of the meadow stood a deer with large antlers. He was grazing on the green grass. Since he was far away and I was involved in drawing close to Spirit, I gave him little heed.

Then as I was returning from my walk I saw that he was much closer. Those antlers looked even larger. I stopped and watched him. He was also watching me, apparently not afraid of me at all. Suddenly, for no apparent reason, he started prancing towards me. My first thought was that perhaps he hadn't seen me. But this couldn't be for he was looking right at me.

As he got closer I realized that indeed he saw me, for now he was glaring at me and throwing his head about. Suddenly I flashed back to an experience my son David once had with a deer at Yosemite. When he attempted to pet it through the open window of our car, the deer reared up and struck the car door a terrific blow. That memory made me a bit more concerned about the situation.

So I did something I've done before when encountering unfriendly animals: I stopped and turned squarely to him. Then raising myself up to my full stature, I shouted for him to stop. He slowed down and finally came to a halt thirty feet before me. For a moment he glared at me, snorted, and threw his head around again. Then turning about, he loped away a few yards. He stopped and looked back at me. Once again he loped several yards before stopping and turning. He repeated this maneuver several more times before he pranced off into the woods.

This morning's episode with the deer reminds me of the time when forty or fifty cows charged down on me from a hill. When I saw I had no place to go, I ran at them shouting and clapping my hands. For a moment it looked as if an unavoidable collision was going to occur, with me the loser. But then suddenly they split ranks: One group veered off to the right while the other went left. Soon they all had disappeared over the hill.

Tuesday, January 24

This morning as I sat on a rock looking out at the ocean, I realized I saw everything as a blur, as a haze, despite the beautiful, bright, blue-skied day. Then quite consciously I began "waking up." I began to become attentive to the things around me and later to the things inside me. At first it was quite a battle breaking through, but after a while everything outside and inside me came into better focus, much like the focusing of a camera. And the dullness, the haze, the fuzziness began to disperse. The colors and light, the sounds of the day became clear and beautiful once more. Now I felt a fuller sense of the energy again.

One thing I noticed during this "awakening" was that the stream of images and thoughts which flit unnoticed across one's mental screen were diminished, almost gone. I think these thoughts and images—which have been termed the stream of consciousness—are so many times the cause of our feelings of dullness and pall, depression and despair, and even sickness. The constant flow of images seem to hypnotize us into believing something about ourselves which is entirely illogical and false.

When I examine this stream of consciousness I see that it operates as a Suggestion Bank which dispenses negative views, ideas, and feelings about ourselves, other people, and the world. (Could it be that everything negative and dark originates from this Bank?) We

human beings, the unsuspecting victims, listen to the words and feel the feelings and think the thoughts that are given us and, believing that they're true, we act upon them or react to them or give in to them.

The classic case of acting upon such negatives is found with the murderer who explains that God told him to kill. If most of us heard such words, we would recognize them as ridiculous if not actually evil and we would dismiss them from our minds. But we're not so apt to dismiss the voice which suggests to us that we're going to be sick or depressed or afraid. Why not? If we did dismiss such thoughts, would we ever suffer from them?

Wednesday, January 25

This morning while out on the beach I felt every human thought and feeling begin to let go. And as they did I began to drop deeper into Spirit and Spirit's joy. It felt as if everything inside me was melting away into the warmth of the energy and the joy of the energy.

After a while I sat down on a rock. The melting and

joy continued to grow. What peace. What harmony was in the joy. What words can ever describe moments like these? Time had stopped and I was seeing everything, feeling everything from a sense of eternity, from a sense of eternal peace where one could stay for hours without moving and be totally contented.

As I looked at a strand of red kelp floating just beneath the surface of the water, I realized I was seeing it with different eyes and from a place other than this world of time, space, and matter. That piece of kelp swaying back and forth contained all the beauty and love that there is; or rather, the place from where I was seeing contained all the beauty and love that there is. Thus what I was seeing was totally beautiful and lovely.

As the process went on, every irritation I'd ever known, every sense of anxiety, frustration, anger, and fear I'd ever felt, every disharmony I'd ever experienced dissolved away. Love was full. I was literally living in love. And from this love I could look at the people nearby and love them. I could look at the gulls and those tiny creatures crawling in the tide pools at my feet and love them. I could look at the world with its horrendous grief and suffering and feel love pouring out to it. Because of the energy of love, I could love beyond all measure of human loving.

Saturday, January 28

I took a few hours off from writing and business today to sit in the courtyard in the sun and read. It's great fun sometimes to read of simpler times—when the Thoreaus and Emersons, the Channings and Carlyles lived. My life, though uncomplicated in comparison with most, seems to simplify even more when I read their words, or when I read their biographies. I enjoy putting myself into their era, into their shoes, into their excellence. They wanted to live life greatly, they wanted to live above and beyond the meanness of daily life. This is uplifting.

One of my favorite books is *Walden*. And some of my favorite reading is a good biography of Thoreau. I love the way Thoreau saw and described nature; he saw it as the closest manifestation of God which we on earth could ever experience. Consequently, we could learn from nature, we could be edified by nature, and we could draw close to God through nature.

I see nature similarly. Nature for me is a resting ground where I can go and find solitude to be with Spirit. It is a reactionless place where the innocence of nature-life can meet the innocence of Spirit's life.

Many people consider Thoreau a pantheist. Surely at times he appeared to be, but there were also many times when he saw nature as secondary to that whole and loving *state of being* which he sought all his life. He once wrote that what was ultimately important to him wasn't nature itself, but rather the soaringness of spirit which results from his closeness with nature. Surely, this soaringness of spirit, this beingness he was describing, was his participation with the energy of Spirit.

Thoreau's was a life filled with happiness and sometimes ecstasy, but also fraught with depression, sickness, pain, and despair. His was a life I have learned from.

Sunday, January 29

To look at the trees, the mountains, the green grasses covering the hills, the yellow flowers by the side of the road—to watch these things without a movement of thought is to be in communion with life; it is to feel that closeness with nature; it is to love.

To look within and feel not the least stirring of thought or feeling is to sense a wholeness within, a unity, a harmony, a contentment. In this too there is love.

Behind and below and above and beyond this love one detects a greater love. This love, a universal love, is vast beyond all comprehension. It is pure because it's untouched by any worldly thing. It is eternal because it has no involvement with time. Time is a condition of the human mind, not of this love. This love is always eternally existing in the now. Thus with love there is none of the sorrow that time brings and none of the pain which man is constantly involved with.

In speaking of this love, which came today when my mind and being were totally harmonious, all I can say in truth is that it is. It exists. To define it further is to become caught in words, which removes me from the experiencing.

Tuesday, January 31

I've been considering tonight the many different ways we've looked at Jesus. We've thought that he was our personal savior; we've thought that he was the son of God; we've thought that he was a spiritual genius or a great man; we've thought that he was Elijah, a prophet, and even God himself; but I don't think we've often perceived Jesus as a person showing us how to be in contact with Spirit. If we did, perhaps our whole impression of him and his message would change.

I understood so much better the meaning of being reborn into Spirit—the words Jesus used when speaking to Nicodemus—the day I thought I was going to die.

When the energy surged into me there was actually a rebirth from matter into Spirit. Jesus didn't mean this metaphorically. It's real. And it doesn't have to happen the way it happened with me. It can occur by just feeling Spirit and yielding one's life to it.

Jesus' words and actions helped me immensely in the overcoming of cancer. His use, for example, of rebuking was something I learned from and used often. It was said by a magistrate of that era that Jesus' rebuke "was fearful." This indicated that he used a tremendous amount of force, a tremendous amount of power when he rebuked. So I began to do the same, with some amazing results.

One of my first experiences with rebuking came while I was back east on business. I had taken time off to play golf with friends. As I was walking to a tee, I inadvertently stepped into a depression in the ground and gave my ankle a terrible twist. I heard the ligaments in my foot give way. Seeing that I was hurt, my friends insisted that I get into the golf cart and get back to the clubhouse. I refused because I knew I had to work this thing out right away with the energy or I'd be suffering major consequences. So, I started walking—limping badly—toward the next green.

The pain was excruciating and the foot and leg had already swelled up to double their size. Since I couldn't direct—I couldn't get that close to Spirit because of the pain—I did the only thing possible: I rebuked. I did so by saying silently, "This is not true." I used these words because I could still recognize that the pain and swelling weren't true in Spirit's world.

I rebuked with as much strength as I could muster. At first nothing happened. And then after a while I felt the pain begin to lessen and the swelling diminish. The leg getting smaller was amazing to watch.

Within twenty minutes things were much better. Even

my friends noticed that I was walking without much of a limp. Before we were back to the clubhouse, I realized that almost all the pain was gone and my foot and leg were almost normal size. Now I was walking quite easily. By evening there wasn't a bit of pain or swelling.

The root of the word *rebuke* means to beat back. This is exactly the feeling I have when I'm rebuking. The feeling is that I'm beating back the symptoms which are the sensations causing the problem.

One of the beautiful things that happens through rebuking is that a mental force is developed which seems to burst through the bonds of matter. This gets one back into that realm or ground of Spirit.

Thursday, February 2

I sit alone this morning and feel a disharmony, an agitation, a sense of isolation both within and without. Eventually, I realize I can release these feelings to the energy. As I do, the harmonious energy begins to absorb the disharmonious feelings. Soon joy is there again.

Matter's disharmonious sensations have no connection to a source. Therefore, these sensations are isolated, conflictive, agitated, unresting. When I feel these sensations, the first response is to react to them, which tends to pull me into their maelstrom thus making me agitated, isolated and unrestful.

But when I'm more alert and I give up these feelings to the energy, they are absorbed by the energy and all conflict eventually disappears. Now I'm connected to a Source. I know it because I can feel it. And because this Source is one, unitary, whole, then I who am now participating with it feel complete. Because I am complete, I feel a unity with everything about.

Friday, February 3

As I look at the many religious teachers, theologians, philosophers, mystics, gurus, who have told us how to be in contact with God, I realize that all methodology must be questioned, for methodology implies a complexity in finding God—rules to follow, techniques to be applied, disciplines to be practiced. In all this, we can become confused and forget that God, Spirit, is simply at hand. Because It is, there's no method for finding It. There's only a yielding of one's life to It.

Saturday, February 4

The kingdom of God isn't within. It's with God. We do, however, feel it within when we've yielded to God, Spirit. Perhaps this is what Jesus was pointing out—that feeling God inwardly is the best and easiest way for us to recognize and identify God.

Sunday, February 5

I think it's *being* that experiences the energy; our being or beingness which has been cloaked by the mind and senses. This beingness is my true sense of life—my eternal life—which emerges and becomes a reality when the mind and senses are in abeyance. This causes me to realize that upon physical death each and every person, no matter how evilly they have lived, will experience the energy, for without that which keeps us from love there will be nothing to obstruct us from love.

Is it fair and just that the evil person and the good person share the same harmonious and perfect life after death? Surely not in our eyes and according to our estimations of fairness and justice. But in God's eyes, in the eyes of Love, I'm sure it's ultimate justice.

Sunday, February 12

As I look at this thing of matter-sensing, I realize that the matter sense of life permeates the whole physical universe. Every physical object we see speaks of matter-sensing and therefore of eventual disharmony. Thus this sense can be looked at as having created the physical universe, or if not having created it, at least it's this universe's essential feature.

Whether or not this sense is the force behind physical creation, the fact is that the five human senses confirm the material world. Spirit doesn't, the senses do. And in this world are objects, animate and inanimate, which are often clothed in natural beauty. But this beauty is short-lived. For everything, because of matter's time-based laws, eventually wilts, decays, dies. So many of us view this process beneficently because matter is all we think there is. But when we feel the energy of Spirit, we begin to realize that there's another universe where love, harmony, and deathlessness are the realities of existence.

Monday, February 13

We're involved in a number of cases of healing, one of which involves a woman with cancer of the spine. We spoke to this lady yesterday and she said that she was feeling much better. I asked her what caused the big changeover from a few days ago when she'd said she was in bad shape. She replied that doubt had left her and she now knew that she was going to be well.

I remember years ago when I first experimented with

healing. It was with the little birds I fed on the front porch of my house. When they didn't see the window and hit it hard, they would usually flip over on their backs and die. But, I found, this could be reversed if I got to them soon enough and told them that they were going to be all right. The important thing was for me to know this through feeling the energy and through feeling their little beings as part of Spirit. It was amazingly beautiful how these words, along with sending the energy to them, would heal their little bodies.

Later as I experimented with my children when they were sick, the results were similar. I remember when Craig (John's son) rode a bicycle without brakes down our steep driveway and smashed into a truck. The force of the blow was so great that his head made a large dent in the truck's door. When I got to him his face was white. The people standing around him were telling each other and Craig how bad he looked. And he did look bad.

After moving the people back, I looked him square in the eyes and told him that he was going to be all right. As I directed the energy to him, I kept asking him if he knew this. Finally he nodded that he did know. The color in his face began slowly to return to normal and his tensed-up body began to relax. On the way to the hospital I held his head in my lap. I kept assuring him that everything was O.K. By the time we arrived the swelling on his head was almost gone. The X-rays confirmed that there was nothing wrong.

Wednesday, February 15

You drive up a road which follows a stream and on into the hills. Along the way are several steer eating by the side of the road. You stop your car and watch them.

One of the animals is at arm's length from your face.
Immediately there's an intimacy with him. You see that
he can't figure out this thing, the car, or the face that's
looking from the car window. He keeps staring at you.
He has a clump of grass hanging from his mouth. After
awhile he becomes assured that there's no danger, so he
resumes chewing.

What a lovely face this animal has. How gentle his
eyes. How almost human his countenance. He reaches
up toward an overhanging branch and scratches his
head. He enjoys the relief from the biting flies which in-
terminably infest his body. He shows enjoyment by closing his eyes as he scratches and snorts. Now he's totally
comfortable next to the car. Giving one last scratch, he
goes back to grazing.

If we really looked at the animals we kill for food,
we'd be more reluctant to participate in this brutality. If
we really looked at them and by so looking got into
their skins a bit, we'd be more aware of what it means
to eat meat. It's because we don't look that we treat

these animals so cruelly and as only objects for our use. If we didn't have enough food from other sources, then there would be some justification for killing animals. But in this country that is just not the case.

The killing of these animals, whether or not we ourselves do it, hardens us to the horror of the slaughterhouse and the hunt.

Thursday, February 16

To realize that Spirit is outside me—is other than me—can be an immense help in letting go of myself, for then I become aware that I must be quiet, I must get out of the way, I must be sensitive, I must be in a state of open expectancy if I'm to sense this other life beyond and above my life. There's really no more to be done if one wants to experience Spirit.

Saturday, February 18

I wonder whether all deep discoveries are "given." Einstein claimed that every great discovery he made came to him spontaneously and unexpectedly. So many writers, musicians, artists, inventors, scientists say that their inspirations and discoveries came from a source beyond themselves. This source they might term the Muse, God, the unconscious, but always it's transcendent to themselves, or if not transcendent then it comes from a place that the self is not consciously aware of.

This morning something beautiful was given to me. I had awakened feeling terrible—achy, feverish, with an upset stomach. Instead of staying in bed, I got up and walked around the room. Immediately my head began throbbing and I became very dizzy. Everything told me to get back in bed, but I've found this only makes matters worse. So I got dressed and went down to the beach.

After walking a while, I sat down on a mound of sand. As I was staring out at the ocean and feeling very ill the thought suddenly arose for me to let go of my body entirely. Even though I'd done this many times before when dealing with illness, it had the ring of newness, the ring of being given, the ring of being the right solution for the present problem.

So following the lead, I got up and started again up the beach. At first it was tremendously difficult to let go of the body, for the body felt wound up like a spring; it felt as if the body was trying to protect itself from the pain by keeping itself tight and tense. But as I kept at it, slowly but decidedly, I began to feel my muscles, bones, sinew—everything—gradually release. And as they did the aches and pains gradually diminished. Now with some encouragement, I worked even harder. Soon I started to feel much better, more energized and stronger. And I was beginning to sense more of the energy of Spirit.

As I observed the process from the "outside," I found my walking was now much more relaxed and released. I saw that this was happening because the body's energy was gone to a great extent and the energy of Spirit was more full within me. I saw that within the energy there were no pain nor hurts nor feverish sensations. Within the energy all was untouched by anything negative. It was totally positive. It was pure perfection.

My focus now was on the dominant feeling—the energy. Thus, my mind was not on the body. In fact as I glanced at the body, I saw it was filled with feelings of well-being, harmony. Words can never describe this feeling.

By the time I was back at the house I felt much better. Within a short while every symptom was gone.

Sickness, I feel, is simply a matter of the senses intensifying. Surely my fever was the intensification of body temperature. And the aches and pains were the intensification of the body's normal sensations.

If viruses cause disease, which is the common assumption, how could a change of sensation, like what happened today, bring about a quick, total healing? The flu virus certainly wasn't destroyed by my feeling the energy. Or was it?

And what about health? What is health? Maybe there's no such thing as actual bodily health. The body may feel better at certain times than at other times, but this is only temporary. Perhaps real health is found and abounds only in this sense of life which is harmony.

This morning I saw distinctly the difference between the body's will and the will of the energy. The body's will is centered in the mind which gives the body commands—lift your arm, move your leg, get up, sit down. These commands are carried out by the body's muscles and nerves.

In contrast to this is the working of the energy. The energy's will is centered in love—in the suchness and beingness of this quality of life. Love simply is and functions within this isness. Love can, however, govern the body if we yield the will of the body—the mind, the thought, the senses—to love. With this yielding of the body an incredible transformation takes place, for the command center of the body changes locations. The energy of love now is the command center. The energy takes control and issues the bodily commands. And these commands are all harmonious. Love fills the body with health, vitality, power. What a way to live!

Wednesday, February 22

There's a small pond in a peaceful field where I love

131

to go and sit. This morning the sun was warm and bright. A gentle breeze whispered through the surrounding oaks and the solitude within and without was immense.

To see, there must be a quiet mind. This morning my mind was very still. I saw the tens of spiders on the water's surface scurrying about searching for a morsel of food. I saw the tiny water bugs spurt up from the muddy bottom to grasp a breath of air. I saw a fish here and there cutting the pond's mirror-surface, creating circles of ripples which would continue reaching out until they arrived at the water's edge. All these things I saw and so much more in the solitude of a moment which had no time, of a moment filled with eternity, of a moment when there wasn't a thought to disturb the peace-filled silence.

Sunday, February 26

My son Craig and a friend of his visited us over the weekend. Craig and I have almost always been close, and the older he gets the closer we become. We get closer not only because he has a good and beautiful heart, but because increasingly he's experiencing love. Consequently, we share together in love.

Today we all went for a long walk. The path through the woods is used solely by the rancher who owns the land. He seldom comes this way since the cows prefer the abundant meadow grass to the sparse grass growing amongst the trees.

After a while, at the far end of the woods, we came across a graveyard. As we wandered about looking at the grave markers, some of which dated back to the 1850s, I remarked about the pain that each of these markers represented for the family, friends, and loved ones who were left behind. "When you realize," I said,

"that this is only a small portion of the tremendous grief, sorrow, pain, shock and horror that's felt daily in the world, then it makes you think about the meaning of this world."

Craig pondered my words for a few moments and then said, "I don't know why God created us to live a while and then to suffer and die."

"What makes you think God created us?" I asked.

"Well, didn't he?"

"I don't see how a loving God could have created a world of suffering and death," I responded.

"Then why are we here?"

"What do you think?"

He thought for several moments and said, "I really don't know. It seems there must be some purpose for us."

"Why couldn't we have just spontaneously generated from matter as the material evolutionists believe?" I asked. "Why should we assume that God created the material universe."

"But if God didn't create the world, then this life is

meaningless," Craig responded. "Also what you're im-
plying is that this life is it; that when you die, you're
dead. And that's the end."

"You know, Craig, I'm not saying that. I know there's
a realm of joy and love beyond this material world.
That energy or life to me is God. That to me is truth.
That to me is heaven to be lived right here on earth."

"But how do the billions of people who live in the
world find that realm?"

"That's the central question of life isn't it? And that's
why I write books, for I really believe that not to come
across that other realm is to miss the whole meaning of
life. But living without that love is the way most people
in the world exist, mainly because they have no choice.
Most people in the world have to spend all their time
and effort just trying to survive, just trying to endure.
So the question of how to come across this other realm
is reserved, for the most part, for the people who have
some leisure, for the people who have the desire to consider issues beyond mere survival and worldly gain."

"But most of us, even when we get more leisure to
consider the deeper issues of life, never take advantage
of it," Craig said. "We don't, I think, because when life's
going pretty well we're too involved with having a good
time."

"Yes, it seems that the only time many of us are interested in finding love or finding God or getting serious
about life is when the walls of sickness, accident, or
some other form of pain come crashing down on us."

"So what are we to do? What's the world to do?"
Craig asked.

"Most people will do what they have always done:
survive and endure until the end. But for myself, I want
this thing we call Love, God or Spirit, with all my heart,
with all my being, with everything that's in me. I'm
burning for it because it's life. This other stuff to me

isn't life. Therefore I actively seek out spirit's life moment by moment. I hardly ever forget about this thing which for me is the heart of life, the heart of joyous and creative living; it's the heart of all help we can give others; it's the heart of eternal life. It *is* eternal life because there's no death in this life."

"But you're talking about living a life above the life we find here," Craig said. "Most people can't do that, nor would they wish to, for they think this life does have ultimate meaning."

"Again, Craig, this world of material sensation and material thought has little meaning for me; it has little meaning because I know there's a different way to live. And this different way is to live with a sense of energy which comes not from me but from a different source. This energy is a life set apart. It's a life transcendent to the pain and suffering of matter-existence. This isn't a belief or a concept; this is a reality which can be experienced, as you know, Craig."

As we headed back, Craig stopped and gazed down at an outcropping of rocks and several granite gravemarkers standing just inside the cemetery fence. "You know," he said, "the deader a thing is, the longer it exists. The more alive something is, like man and the animals, the more vulnerable it is to death and decay."

Tuesday, February 28

Many traditional psychologists maintain that we are the products of our past experiences. They say the past is who we are and we can't change this; we can alter the negative effects of our past experiences through various forms of therapy, but we can't change the fact that we are the past.

Most of the creative people I've known and read

about realize that one must be free somewhat from the past, for the past keeps one from being with the new, from feeling the new, from seeing life anew. This, the new, is the nature of creativity; it's the meaning of the word creativity. Thus to carry our old and worn past with us only serves to block out the new.

So what is the new and how does it come about? I think it can only come about through letting go of the old, which is myself, for the self, it seems, is the reservoir of my past experiences, my history, my memory. Thus by letting go, my past is cut off. And with this I'm automatically with the new.

The energy of love is the new. It's that quality which is the essence of creation. Love is endlessly new. Love always sees life afresh. Love sees the wholeness of life with its joy and beauty, with its sorrow and pain, with its conflicts and pleasures. Love sees the meaninglessness of a life lived without love.

To live with the new—with love—constantly, this is the height and depth of creativity. This is joy and bliss. This is the only eternal life there is.

Friday, March 2

Last night I awakened in the middle of the night with extreme pain in my Achilles' tendon. Getting up to test things, I found I could barely stand. Immediately the thought jumped out that I'd injured the tendon while playing tennis. Instinctively, I reached down and touched the painful area. It was swollen to several times its normal size. For a while I worked with the energy, directing against the pain, and since the foot began to feel better I went back to sleep.

Today I awoke with the foot somewhat better, but still there was swelling and quite a bit of soreness. Since

I had a busy day I didn't really work to heal it until I went out for a walk in the late afternoon. As I was walking—limping really, quite severely—down to the pond I began to let go of the body. Immediately the energy increased and I began directing it toward my foot.

After a while I realized that within the energy which I was feeling and directing was great power. Along with this came the realization that within the painful foot was a great sense of weakness. I saw that if in the place of that weakness I could begin to feel strength and power, then the foot would be healed.

Keeping this insight in mind, I began to direct powerfully toward the foot—I literally drove the energy into that area. With each surge of energy I felt my foot strengthen, solidify. It began to move more freely and support the weight of my body more easily. And I wasn't feeling the power just in my foot; I was feeling it throughout my body.

Now it felt as if I wasn't so much walking on a sore foot as walking on the strength and firmness of the energy. By the time I got to the pond I was well on my way toward freedom from the pain. And by the time I had walked up from the pond and was back at my car, almost all the pain and swelling were gone.

Sunday, March 4

As I sat in his bedroom so many times directing the energy to his cancer-wracked body, despite his semiconsciousness, he'd wake up and smile. He wouldn't be smiling at me, for often he wouldn't know I was in the room. But smile he did and often. And I recall thinking that somehow and in some way the energy was reaching him.

137

The energy did reach both him and his wife, I found out later. His wife, who recently came over for dinner, said quite matter of factly, "Oh yes, I felt the energy often. And I know my husband did too. Sometimes he'd wake up and say 'John's here.' And when I'd tell him, 'No, John isn't here now,' he'd smile and say 'Oh yes he is.' "

Wednesday, March 7

Picasso once said that when he entered his studio to create he left his body outside the door much like a Moslem leaves his shoes outside the mosque. Mahler, Mozart, and Beethovan spoke of leaving the human realm and entering a different realm of life while they were composing. Balzac, Goethe, and a host of other writers have said similar things. Artists throughout history have recounted that the creative process involves leaving self behind.

The experience of leaving self behind and being in touch with Creation is, I believe, one which most of us have had. Probably as children we felt the touch of Creation, but as we got older we forgot it because we got caught up in the world of self-conscious thinking and concerns; we got caught up in the world's sense of life.

So the question is for some of us: Can we get back in contact with Creation? This poses a second question: Can we find a way to die to the world's sense of life right now while we're living here on earth? For with the death of this sense, then the other sense of life—Spirit's sense—is there.

Upon touching that realm, we may not write a book or paint a picture, or sculpt a work of art, but we will find what we may have been seeking—peace, joy, harmony, and love.

Mozart reported that his state of mind while creating was like a vivid dream. Goethe said that while he was writing *The Sorrows of Werther* he felt like a somnambulist. Brahms said that when he was at his creative best he was in a dream-like state.

So many artists have described their times of creation as dream-like or close to sleep. This state evidently allows creativity to flourish, new ideas to spring forth. I think this is because when one's in that state where life appears much like a vivid dream, the conscious mind is in abeyance.

I've noticed, at times, that when I've begun to feel Spirit quite deeply, I might begin to get somewhat drowsy. I believe this is just the natural outcome of the yielding of the body and the mind. But sleep is not what I or the artist seek. What is being sought is the Creative Source. So when a Brahms's mind slows down—as he himself has stated—and he feels himself drifting out of the conscious world, he becomes aware of what is happening in the World of Creation. And he attends to the sounds, to the themes, to the ideas and intuitions that are there but which are normally blocked out when the mind is focused on the conscious elements of life.

This realm of life, this Source of Creation the artist is touching upon is, I believe, Spirit's realm. Brahms seems to agree. He said that when he was at his peak of creativity—when he was being given themes to record— he felt he was in a ". . . soul-realm, a spiritual state. This is where all creation takes place."

The other day an artist, whom I just happened to meet while on a walk, opened up and told me that he had an experience of real joy years ago which occurred while he was strolling alone in a forest. He said he doesn't know why it happened, but he does know that it was the only real experience of his life.

More and more I find people relating such experiences. I wonder why, if these experiences of joy are so real to them, more people aren't searching out ways to be in contact with this joy? Perhaps it's because they don't know how to begin to search for it, or perhaps it's that their lives are so busy that they don't have the time.

Yet there may be another factor, a major factor. I know there was for me and for others. And that factor is that when we really got serious and dedicated to seeking out joy daily, we were met and temporarily blocked by a resistance which we've termed negative energy. This resistance often came in the form of discouragements, disruptions, distractions, disappointments, and sometimes sickness.

To be aware that we may be met with resistance can, I feel, be a tremendous help in moving forward with Spirit. For if and when resistance does crop up, then we'll see the importance of dealing with it immediately. And when we do, we'll find that nothing can ever stop us from moving ever more deeply into the kingdom of joy which is really the kingdom of God.

Thursday, March 8

A young man asked the other day how he could experience the energy more frequently. "Right now," he said, "the only time I feel the energy is when I'm listening to beautiful music."

"Why only with music?" I asked.

"Because I just get lost in the beauty,"

"Getting lost to self-consciousness," I said, "is perhaps the only way to sense the energy. And learning how to get lost is an ongoing exploration for everyone who desires to live with love."

When a friend asked Thoreau, as he lay dying, how the "opposite shore" looked to him, Thoreau's reply was: "One world at a time."

I believe as Thoreau did that if we keep focused on this world—try to live here with as much caring, compassion, and love as possible—then the hereafter will take care of itself.

I talked today to a woman whose mind dwelt constantly on the hereafter. And this is understandable for she's lonely and unhappy. So to avoid thinking about these things, she continually contemplates the joy she'll someday have in heaven.

I could have said something to her about focusing on the present and trying to deal with her problems now. But that would have been cruel, for I really think she's doing the best she can. Perhaps all of us are doing the best we can. After all, we are all seeking happiness and completeness in our many different ways.

While sitting at a pond this morning and after having worked for others, I began thinking about all the things I had to do, along with several business concerns and a particular disturbance which has been going on right next to my home. So after figuring, mulling, thinking for awhile, I finally awoke to the fact that all these things could be handled by Spirit. It wasn't my responsibility to take action—if indeed any action was required—from a thinking base which is always a limited way of acting. Instead, I could let go and give the problems to Spirit, knowing that Spirit's answers and directions would be

the ultimate in intelligence. In fact, Spirit's answers, as I've discovered so many times before, would incorporate solutions I had never thought about, because it's scope of perception is unbounded. As the mind functions within the realm of time which is limitation in itself, Spirit's intelligence functions within the sphere of eternity which is infinitude in itself.

What a relief! Now I knew, because I could feel it, that Spirit was in control. It was Spirit's "problem" now, not mine. And because it was, I knew that the solutions to the problems would be taken care of in a fashion infinitely more creative and harmonious than I could ever devise.

When handling problems this way, I've found it extremely important—imperative really—to be ready and willing to take all forms of action when the insight to act has been given. Not to act is not to trust the guidance. One will know whether the action indicated is from

Spirit or not by the quality of harmony contained within the insight. Also, if it's not the right action, then we'll find ourselves stopped, in some way, by Spirit

Thursday, March 22

Dr. Henry Hitt Crane (formerly a Methodist minister at a large church in downtown Detroit) probably had more to do with my early seeking for God than any other person. I'll never forget a Sunday sermon he preached on love and loving others. As I listened to him, I kept asking myself, "But how do I love? I don't feel love inside. What I do feel is agitation, anxiety, and the pressure to succeed in this world so I can provide for my family and myself."

Still, his message took. Contained within his question of how we can love was the possibility of loving. And he, I saw, did love; he did care for people, he did give of himself, he did lose himself in his giving. His way of loving was just to do it. "A baby doesn't ask how to walk, he just does it. Likewise, we can just love," he said.

Dr. Crane's capacity to love sprang, I believe, from that tremendous, dynamic energy which ran through his whole being. He was vitally alive and every gesture, every look on his face, every word he spoke reflected his aliveness. He was a living dynamo whose energy seemed to integrate his being and raise him above the world and place him in that other world of love.

I shall always be grateful to Dr. Crane for his early help and tutelage. Mostly, I'm grateful for the person of Dr. Crane: his manner, his actions, his caring, his compassion and deep love for his fellow human beings. These qualities showed me that life could be lived with greatness; they showed me that life could be lived with awareness, with intelligence, with beauty, with courage and, most importantly, with love.

Saturday, March 24

The material senses attest to a material universe. The sense of touch feels matter. The sense of hearing hears the din and song of matter. The sense of sight sees only matter. Smell and taste likewise can sense only matter. These material senses naturally can only sense and perceive their own likeness, which is matter.

But when these senses yield themselves, then another sensing of life—a spiritual sensing—replaces the matter senses. Now with this harmonious sense of life flowing through us we find that, instead of feeling matter so much, we feel Spirit and love. Instead of feeling time so much, we sense eternity. Instead of being caught in the ugliness and despair of the world so much, we feel beauty and joy.

With this harmonious sense dominating our sensing, we can now say that to this sense there is no matter, for this sense is not cognizant of nor does it feel matter's life.

Sunday, March 25

Last evening the energy of Spirit filled all the places where the senses within the body are felt. Soon a state of unacknowledgement, of nonrecognition began to happen. It was as if Spirit in its unknowingness and nonrecognition of this material world erased all my knowing and recognition. The transition had occurred; thought and sensation were gone. And I found my being in that other world.

Caroline and I were wondering about the date we first met, so I looked back in my journals and found it was November 23, 1976. My journal notes remind me of the first impressions I had about this beautiful lady and about the healing she had asked for. The several journal entries read:

> Met Caroline today. She seems so naturally endowed with a spiritual sensing of life. And she seems so interested in what I'm about. Later as we talked she asked for a healing for her back.

And then on November 27, 1976:

> The back healing took place. She said she was standing at her sink doing dishes when all of a sudden this gentle sense of love began to happen in her back. And "then like a creaky old ship, my back just slipped back into place." She asked me what I had done and I told her, "nothing" save seeing—feeling—her through the energy as she truly is: a being of Spirit."

And on November 28 another entry reads:

> I saw Caroline again today as I was coming out of the market. She wants to know "what this thing is." I really think she may be the first one who will go for it. I hope she will. I'll do everything I can to help. And I know Spirit will help her.

Eight years later we know that she did "go for it." Despite all the battles—the ups and downs, the disruptions and sometimes discouragements, the dealing with evil and the evolving recognition that there really is no evil—she kept with Spirit. And now today Spirit truly is her life.

Caroline is the only one of the three of us who has recorded her spiritual odyssey right from the beginning. I think someday these cassette tapes will be classics.

145

As D. H. Lawrence (English author) was dying of tuberculosis he said that he thought his illness was a disease of melancholy. Mary Baker Eddy (the founder of Christian Science) said that tuberculosis and cancer are caused by dark images of the human mind. Dr. Simonton said that so many people he has treated with cancer had dark and traumatic times some months prior to contracting the disease.

All this makes me wonder why more research isn't done on the mental nature of disease. Perhaps it's because there's a fear that such research might undermine the medical profession. But I really think it's more than this. I think that people—doctors, scientists, researchers, laymen—just don't think it's possible that the mind could cause a disease such as cancer. The assumption—the certainty, almost—has been that the body is self-acting. Thus the body has the propensity to get sick without the mind's consent, which I don't think is the case.

There might be still another reason for this reluctance to check the mind/body disease connection: people's fear of being responsible for their illness. I remember reading about a psychologist who had received a grant to investigate whether there was any connection between cancer and the mind. He circulated through hospitals in New York City attempting to interview cancer specialists. To his surprise and chagrin, he found hardly a doctor who would talk to him, and those who did treated him evasively.

Finally, he asked an administrator of a hospital what was going on. This man said, "Do you know what would happen if a link between cancer and the mind were found? Every person who contracted cancer would blame himself for his disease. For most people this would be intolerable. It's much easier for us to think that our disease is caused by a virus than to think that we're in some way responsible for it."

Saturday, March 31

A renowned holistic teacher and healer explained through books, articles, and television appearances that people are responsible for their illnesses. She emphasized that if we become sick it is up to us to rid our mental systems of our resentments, fears, angers, hates—every form of negativity. Then and only then can our bodies be healed.

Recently I read she had cancer. Within several months she had died. How she must have been tortured by her inability to cure herself. It seems that no one answer is the entire answer, and that what works with some people doesn't always work with others.

Monday, April 2

The other night I awoke with an upset stomach. As I lay in bed attempting to get clear, the thought arose, "Where's Spirit?" And I realized immediately that Spirit was outside of me. This immediately released my body and mind from the struggle to do something. With the release I let out a large sigh, and I began to feel my body let go into a state of deep relaxation—actually a state beyond relaxation. As this was happening, I felt an influx of love, of softness, of lightness, of healing. What a tremendous thing it is to feel the hurting areas of one's body begin to be comforted. I stayed with the love and lightness for quite some time. In the morning all was well.

Tuesday, April 3

This morning while out on a walk, I asked, "How do I feel *only* the energy?" And the answer which came once more was: Let the energy entirely govern your body and mind in all that you do.

What a challenge to let the energy govern one's whole being, for matter with its force and sensations and thoughts would like to control one and dictate how one should think, act, and feel. It takes a constant alertness, a constant awareness, to constantly let go of self.

Saturday, April 7

Today would have been my brother's fifty-seventh birthday. Instead it marks, almost to the day, his death eighteen years ago. What a tragedy his death was, as most deaths are, not only a tragedy in the way he died, but because he was beginning to come into his own. He was beginning to consider the deeper issues of life rather than being so totally focused on making a living, raising a family, and surviving.

Also, for the first time in a long while my brother and I could talk, we could discover together, we could share together. We finally became friends, which we hadn't been for years. Before, we hardly ever communicated except on superficial issues, and we were quite critical of each other. He always thought I was too open, too eclectic in my approach to life. I thought he was too rigid, too steeped in that conservative religious thinking of his. So just as we were coming together and relating better, just as he was starting to be happier and more content within himself, the cancer struck. What a waste. What a carnage it wrought on his family, our parents, his friends, and on me who began, once more, to love him deeply.

Sunday, April 8

What aspect of Spirit brings about instantaneous healings? I've asked this question for years. Now perhaps I have an answer: It's the quality of what I would call the *spiritual sensing within the body.*

The body certainly senses life materially. Almost everyone, I think, would agree. This material sensing of life is what causes every physical problem. Now if the body can somehow yield this sensing, then the other sense—the spiritual sense—will begin to infuse the body. And it's this which can bring about an instantaneous physical healing. This has happened to me twice in recent weeks.

I first got a glimpse of the potency of this sensing of Spirit about a month ago when I was having a physical problem. Through directing and releasing the body to Spirit, especially the troubled area, I was able to keep things at bay, but still the problem went on.

Then one morning, feeling more discomfort than usual, I got up and went into the den. I was seeking for an insight. I really needed an insight. As I sat in my reading chair, it suddenly came to me to yield the hurting, disharmonious sense I was feeling to the harmonious sense of Spirit. So I began gently to yield the discordant feeling, and immediately I felt a gentle, peaceful sense of Spirit infusing that whole area. Right in the place where a moment before I had felt discomfort, I now sensed harmony, peace, a gentle love. It felt as if that sense had been waiting just outside my body to come into me when I had yielded sufficiently.

149

There was scarcely a doubt now that I was healed. Actually it really didn't matter whether I was healed right then, for I knew if I weren't, it would soon be forthcoming. And, because of the gentle peace and contentedness I was feeling, it really didn't matter that much what the body was doing.

As things turned out I was healed. The amazing thing is that though the discomfort seemed so strong, so powerful, so impossible to be healed except through massive doses of Spirit, actually it was the gentlest feeling of Spirit I perhaps have ever felt that healed the problem.

My second recent instantaneous healing was about a week ago. We had gone to a friend's house for dinner. Somewhere along the way the hostess's son made mention that he was on antibiotics because of a bad sore throat and laryngitis. I didn't think much about his comment since he looked fine. I did notice though as we were about to leave that he was sweating profusely.

We got home about midnight and went to bed. In the night I awoke with a very sore throat. Immediately I thought of the young man and contagion. Then my thoughts flashed back to all those times years ago when I'd had a similar problem and had to spend several days nursing a swollen throat and laryngitis. The thoughts decended upon me before I knew it. That's what alerted me that now was the time to work.

As I began to direct, a thought again flashed, this one about how long it was going to take to overcome this problem. But this time the thought didn't take root, for immediately the realization dawned that I could just gently yield the sensation of inflammation and let the healing energy flow into that area. I did just this, and immediately the feeling of Spirit's gentle presence entered my body and filled that place of discomfort. Now I could feel the soreness begin to fade away much as a cloud disperses with the coming of the breeze. Within a minute or two all of the soreness was gone. This healing, in a way, was even more amazing than the other because I could watch the feeling of soreness just fade away.

Monday, April 9

As I've been experimenting with this different sensing of Spirit, I find that it's better if the yielding of the disharmonious sense is done easily and gently rather than vigorously or with a spontaneous release, for the gentle yielding seems to invite that gentle sensing of Spirit. This, the gentle sensing, is the quality which heals when infusing the body.

Since this way of sensing Spirit feels like a Presence, I've been wondering and asking what it's a presence of. I believe it might well be the presence of my eternal spiritual identity which has been covered up, primarily by the human senses, and is revealed when these senses have yielded themselves.

Thursday, April 12

I don't think I've ever felt so deeply that there's another person of Spirit living right in the place where the material human being is. This realization has been dawning on me all day long. Then while I was on a walk the realization grew into untold proportions. Is the person of Spirit the real one? We can hypothesize, surmise, assume; we can conjecture, conceptualize, believe. But when we actually feel this person, then we know better than we know our own human lives that, yes, this person is the real eternal being made by God.

In speaking about a similar issue, Krishnamurti once said in effect that the Atman or higher self can't be truth, for Atman is the outcome of thought, which makes it a construct of the mind and not of truth. But if one actually feels this self as much as or at times even more than one's physical self, then what is one to do? Reject it. I can't, in all honesty.

I really believe if one is quiet enough and with Spirit enough that this realization will be given to anyone who deeply desires it. It was given me today quite unexpectedly and in a surprising fullness. Tonight as I write this I can say that this person of Spirit is my real identity and thus the real identity of every person, though most of us don't know it. We don't know because the truth of our being has always been covered over.

I think it's important not to dogmatize a position such as the above, for I don't know for sure what's really going on. All I can do is report how it feels, and then, using the clarity of Spirit, try to decipher what's occurring. The danger I want forever to avoid is that of making a thing—the concept, for example, of an eternal spiritual self—more important than the fact of feeling Spirit, for I know how much humanity historically has had this tendency to focus on effects rather than going for the source—God, Spirit—where the real essence of life is found.

Sunday, April 15

This morning I decided to go with what had been given—that is, the gentle infusion of Spirit which I've felt so much since the healings. This was in a way a large decision because I've been bothered by a problem I thought could only be handled by the power of Spirit.

So after having decided, I just resolved to trust Spirit and go with it—just leave things in Spirit's hands and not work so hard myself. The result is that tonight I'm free of the problem and very peaceful.

Tuesday, April 17

There are so many aspects of Spirit. Which one's right? All of them. How Spirit touches our being isn't as important as the recognition that it is Spirit.

I drop away from the body and feel the incredible purity of Spirit, so much so that it's pure heaven. This is the strength and the power of Spirit.

Then I gently yield the bodily senses, and I feel an infusion of Spirit. This is the feeling of being taken care of, for I know that my whole being including the body and mind is part of Spirit.

Two sensings, both a part of that wholeness which is Spirit.

Sunday, April 22

Eternal life, it seems, is the pure energy without the body being involved. Beingness is the energy of love and gentleness infusing the body—it's Spirit coming to earth and notifying humankind that everyone can be filled with the energy despite our sensing of matter.

If Spirit is all around us, then we can understand why attention, releasing the body, yielding the senses, all work to bring about the sensing of the energy. With attention we've used a high state of mental energy to break through the human senses. With the release of the body we've dropped the senses. And through yielding the senses we've allowed what is all around us—Spirit—to infuse that place where we feel the senses. Thus we see again that the senses are the only thing which keeps us feeling separate from Spirit.

We shouldn't let any sensing of Spirit pass and get lost, for it's our being touched by God. And the place where He has touched we can always rerealize and come back to.

Wednesday, April 25

We have a little bird, a starling, which each morning waits on our front deck for us to get up. She stands with feathers all fluffed out staring in through our window. When she sees one of us, she'll start chirping and clicking and pacing back and forth to make sure she gets our attention.

She first appeared one morning as we were having breakfast on the deck. As she came closer, we told her how beautiful she was, and then we threw her a bit of toast. Without hesitating, she grabbed it, flew off a few feet, and then proceeded to dine leisurely on this new-tasting morsel. Before long she was back for more, which she got. Ever since then we've had a friend who lives on our front lawn and often stands on our front rail looking into the den where I work.

When I get up for a bit of coffee or to take a break, she'll make sure she gets noticed with her chirps and her pacing. Right now as I turn to look, I see her standing atop the windbreak. It happens to be the only place from which she can see me and also be seen. So I think

I'll get up and get her a piece of cracker. She likes crackers now much better than toast.

What this little creature likes best of all, I think, is the love she feels. This morning I was a little late getting up, so I hurriedly tossed her a piece of cracker; I always have her crackers standing atop the stereo speaker just inside the front door. Instead of swooping in and grabbing it as she usually does, this time she just stood there looking at me. It was as if she were waiting for some kind of hello, some kind of loving remark, as this is how I usually greet her. So I opened the door and told her how beautiful she was and how much we loved her and loved her coming by each morning. With this, she wobbled over to the food and began eating. Birds, like man, don't live by crackers alone.

Monday, May 21

I'm sitting alone by a river which is roaring past me (they were on a camping trip). The force of the river is

155

incredible. It takes huge limbs of trees and throws them down the river and over large boulders. Right now the sun is just beginning to dip behind a mountain peak some 14,000 feet high.

I went for a walk awhile ago amidst pine trees on a path which few people have ever walked. And I considered again the question: What is real? This question came after much directing toward and releasing the internal feelings in the body. These are perhaps the only witnesses against Spirit. This evening they were dominant enough to be distracting and disruptive to feeling Spirit deeply. But then the energy erased the heavy sense. So the question was formed while I was feeling a depth of eternal life and then looking back at this life. And I asked if the real is of time, of pain and sorrow—that is, of this world—or is the real of the order of bliss and eternal harmonious life?

I feel each one of us, when we are at peace enough and full enough with a rich sense of our own beingness, knows down deep that our eternal, real life is not of this world. Even with the beautiful mountains and joyous streams, even with the most magnificent of nature's scenes, we realize that this is not eternity—the ultimately real for us. We know it because everything of time-based matter eventually declines, decays, dies. And this process, we somehow know, is not our eternal life.

So if this life we find ourselves with and in today is not the eternally real—if it's not ours to be lived in eternally—then how do we realize that life of eternity? For if the life of eternity is real, then there must be a way to live in its reality now, no matter how great the sensing of matter.

We intuit that upon physically dying—dying to the body and its sensations, dying to the physical world with its time-filled "realities"—that all this relativeness stops, all our suffering stops. We intuit that then all will be ecstasy and bliss, for that which has held us in bondage has been dropped. But why not now? Why can't we leave the body's sensations right now and enter that dimension of death—which is not death at all, but life—where time and sorrow are not?

We can. We know we can, for this life of ecstasy is actual. It's actually our eternal life. And being eternal, we can have it right now and right here. How? By letting go of the false—the matter, time-based life—for with the dropping of this, the other appears.

When one finds, one day, that this energy of love is more one's life than the human sense of life, then one may ask: "What is true about myself? Am I a human being who has found this energy, or am I an entity who is part of the energy and who finds himself here as a human being, clothed in the material garments of the world?" The answer to this question is crucial if one is to continue growing in love and overcoming the things which would oppose this life.

EARLIER EPISODES

The following three journal entries record events which occurred prior to 1983, the time when I first began writing *The Healing Energy of Love.* Because these episodes were important in my development and because of the interest I feel they will hold for the reader, I have included them in this section.

The first, a miraculous healing, caused me to realize that Spirit works in ways different from man's logic system and human understanding. It also created in me an impetus to discover how the body could be healed, for I saw how poor bodily health could deter one from seeking out the energy of Spirit.

The second segment deals briefly with my teaching at the Happy Valley School, founded by J. Krishnamurti and Aldous Huxley. This truly was a joyous time for me, for not only had I broken away from the business world—that world for which I was not suited—but I was finally involved in an occupation I was suited for and which I loved.

The last segment tells about my meetings with Krishnamurti, which were enjoyable and educational. Since 1962 when I first read *The First and Last Freedom,** I have had a great respect for Krishnamurti. I

---

*J. Krishnamurti (New York: Harper and Row, 1954, 1975).

158

especially like him because he seems so concerned with this matter of living. He seems deeply dedicated to understanding the cause of humanity's tribulations and sorrow as well as what brings happiness and joy. Since I felt a similar desire to find out about life, I naturally felt a kinship with him.

April 1969

Last night I had a healing for my back. It was really the most miraculous thing that has ever happened to me. It all began as I was about to take Craig and Linda to San Diego for a short vacation.

As I was loading our suitcases in the car and feeling quite elated about our little sojourn, suddenly a terrible pain pierced my back. It literally doubled me up. For a moment I couldn't think or speak. Then, telling the children that I was hurting and needed to lie down for a while, I struggled back up the stairs.

As I lay on the couch wondering how I could ever make the trip, I suddenly thought of the day my brother was buried. As I was standing at the grave next to my dad and mom suddenly my back started hurting in exactly the same way. The pain, like this time, was excruciating and it didn't go away for several weeks. If this was the case again—and it seemed to be—then I just didn't know how we could go. And yet I couldn't disappoint them. We'd all been looking forward to the trip for so long.

Somehow I managed to get down the stairs, into the car, and off we drove. We did swim a bit, and we did get to the zoo, but everything I did was pure agony. It was misery to sit, stand, walk, or try to sleep. By this time I was listing over well to my right because every muscle in my lower back was frozen solid.

By the time the weekend was over and we were back home the situation had worsened. Maybe it was just that I was worn down. In any event for the first time in a long time, as I lay in bed trying to find some relief, I reached out to God and asked for help. I don't know what I expected from the prayer. Perhaps a miracle. But for a long while nothing happened.

And then, just as I started to drift into that zone between wakefulness and sleep, it happened. Suddenly and totally unexpectedly I felt what seemed to be two huge hands grab my lower spine and twist it, first one way, then the other, and then back again the first way. With each twist my back crunched and cracked. My God, I just couldn't believe it. Had it really happened? Yes, it wasn't a dream. It was real. Then it slowly dawned on me that I wasn't feeling any pain. Had I been healed?

For several moments I just lay there. I was shocked, startled. And I was afraid that it might not be true, that I might not be healed. Then very slowly I sat up. No pain so far. I got to my feet. Still no pain. I carefully bent side to side and then a bit forward. Absolutely no pain. My God, I was healed, and in an instant. Miraculously healed! The tears started to come and just kept coming. And in the midst of the tears came words of thanks.

What made the healing happen? Is there any "law" involved? Can I be in that "mood" or inclination so that such healings can occur regularly?

I see now that when those huge hands grabbed me *I* was really out of the way; I was in that state between wakefulness and sleep. Therefore there was no interference on my part. But how can one *intentionally* get out of the way? That implies staying in the way.

And what or whose hands were those? It all seems to point in an anthropomorphic direction. Maybe there is a personal aspect of God which helps us at times. I just don't know. What I do know is that I'm very grateful.

I recall that just before the hands grabbed my back and began twisting, the image of myself was momentarily erased. It was as if my image was on a blackboard; in my mind's eye I actually saw it there. And then something or someone just erased it. I was literally gone for a moment—or rather the image of me was gone for a moment. This leads me to wonder if perhaps the image which we hold of ourselves contains all the pain and sickness which we feel. Thus it may be a major obstacle which needs to be eradicated if we're to have a healing. By eradicating the image, it seems that we've erased self-consciousness, which is the recognition that we have a body and mind separate from God and therefore vulnerable to the onslaughts of pain and disease.

The physical image we have of ourselves is perhaps the only thing that pain and sickness can fasten onto. This image *is* what we call our physical self. Without the physical image I lose awareness of my self-conscious identity, and my other identity—that which is a part of God—is given the opportunity to emerge and be felt.

Is this the right analysis of what happened? I don't know. It all sounds so complicated in view of the simplicity of the healing. Whatever, I'm just so grateful. And why not leave it a mystery? Why do we have to figure everything out?

May 1974

The evening sun is softly touching the mountains around Ojai, creating a purple glow. The calls of crows and the barking of dogs along with the muffled sound of a distant car all fit into the solitude of this moment. And

161

there is the sensing of an infinitude of love, a love which is in the world but whose source, one detects, is beyond the world.

I recall another time several years ago when I looked at these same mountains and contemplated the beginning of a new life, a life so different from before. What a joy it was to teach! What a joy it was to sit on the edge of my desk and look into the eyes of those young people. Most of them really wanted to learn. They were interested. They were enthusiastic about finding out about themselves and the world. What a love affair we developed. I felt so much love for those students; I couldn't have loved my own children any more. And I learned that most of them cared for me. Teaching becomes such an easy matter when you have students and teacher working together like this. Then learning becomes a daily adventure.

I remember one day in class when a student asked me if I thought that by taking drugs one could reach that place of union with God. He asked the question because I'd acknowledged that I'd never taken drugs. Yet I had related experiences I had which were evidently similar to drug-induced experiences.

Instead of answering his question, I asked him

162

whether he thought it was possible to experience an in-finitude of life such as God through finite means such as a drug. Wouldn't such finite means bring about finite ends—that is, visionary experiences, false nirvanas, trance-like and mesmeric states which have nothing to do with God?

He disagreed, saying I couldn't make such a deter-mination since I'd never taken drugs. I admitted he was right, and I congratulated him for not just accepting my answer. I said, however, that I still doubted that one could experience that vast life of Spirit through taking drugs.

I'll never forget my last day in class when I said good-bye. It was quite an emotional experience, for I knew I'd never see most of the students again. I wanted to tell them so much, but all I could say was that I had learned so much from them; I had learned so much more from them than I ever could have taught them. And then I had to leave. My emotions ran too deep.

What I would like to have said was that I had learned from the experiences they shared with me. I had learned from their thoughts, from their insights, from their understandings. I had learned from their caring for each other, just as I had learned from the unkindness they sometimes displayed to each other. Mainly, I had learned more about myself and the world through them; I had learned that all of us are really similar, though we attempt to divide ourselves from each other by maintain-ing that we're separate individuals. The fact is we are very much the same. We all have similar hopes, aspira-tions, wishes, fears, angers, resentments, hurts. We all want to find a sense of happiness, of fulfillment, of com-pleteness. We all want to be able to give and to share and to have compassion for one another. We all want to be able to love.

163

Then I wanted to say that I hoped each one of them would continue to learn all through life. Never get stuck. Keep moving through. Keep asking questions. Keep questioning every concept and every person. Never just accept, believe, take somebody's word for it. Be lovingly skeptical but never cynical.

Finally, I wanted to say that I hoped that somewhere along the way they would learn what it means to be alone, what it means to be in solitude. For all great learning, great insights, great understandings are perhaps given here—in the silence of solitude, in the depths of aloneness. Here perhaps God is found and one's connection to God. Here perhaps they will find what they've always been looking for, even though they haven't known it. Here they may find that joy of life which will always be with them despite the many problems they have yet to face.

All these things I wish I could have said to them. But that day I just couldn't.

February 1978

Today I met with Krishnamurti. Since I was early for the appointment, I wandered about the campus of Pepperdine University which is right across the highway from the home where he was staying.

The setting of the university is exquisite. It looks out at the ocean and has as a backdrop a group of tall, green mountains. I walked to the far edge of the parking lot where I could be alone and sat down on the grass. I wanted to draw as close to the energy as I could before our meeting. I wanted very much for our meeting to have meaning and depth and be a time of discovery. It always seems easier to be close to the energy at times like these, perhaps because the situation requires it. The gulls, the blue ocean, the aloneness all seemed to help bring me more deeply into love's reality.

I parked my car just inside the gate and walked up the long driveway to the house. I had hardly removed my finger from the doorbell when the door opened. A lovely lady with a pleasant smile greeted me. To her right and a little behind stood Krishnamurti. He looked frail, reserved, and was shorter than I had expected.

They invited me in. The living room overlooked a lawn and a garden. Beyond were high cliffs and at the foot of the cliffs was the ocean. The sun glinted brightly off the water making it hard to look at.

Krishnamurti and Mrs Z. inquired about where I lived and what I did. K. seemed somewhat surprised that I had children and had spent a good share of my life in business.

After a while, Mrs. Z. excused herself, leaving K. and me alone. Surmising I had only a limited time, I immediately began talking about awareness. Our understanding of awareness is quite similar. We agreed that the human mind by its very nature couldn't be aware to any great depth. I said I felt that deep awareness is possible only when the energy of life is functioning. We agreed that the awareness from the energy is different in kind and quality from the awareness of the mind. And yet, he said, the mind when not fragmented—when not viewing life from a part of consciousness but from the totality of consciousness—could have an awareness which transcends the brain's limited awareness.

We then discussed how the energy might best be realized and whether such energy comes from us or from a different source. We agreed that the energy is not of the self but can be realized when the self was absent.

What was the best way to arrive at the absentness of

self? Here we moved apart somewhat. K. maintained that it's only through the total silencing of the mind that the self can be abnegated and consequently the "otherness" might be there. I said that a deep inner letting go of the body could also facilitate self-abnegation. I suggested that the body is more involved with the mind's chattering and continuance than most of us realize. The body and mind play off each other and thus perpetuate each others' life, I said. So by short-circuiting the body—by taking away the mind's blackboard, as it were—then the mind must quiet down.

K. disagreed. He thought the body is much like a horse. It does what the mind tells it. But it has a life of its own, an organic life totally separate from the mind. Therefore, the body isn't the important factor in self-abnegation. The mind is.

Our conversation had gone on for over an hour when Mrs. Z returned. I thought that this was the signal for my departure, so I was surprised when K. suggested that Mrs. Z and I get acquainted while he took leave for a while.

For the next fifteen minutes or so, Mrs. Z and I had a cordial conversation. She is a gracious lady, very lovely and beautiful. When K. returned he asked me if I'd like to join a discussion group which would be meeting next month in Ojai. I said that I'd enjoy participating. All in all, our meeting was delightful and enlightening.

March 1978

Just back from a discussion group with Krishnamurti. When I got there, about ten minutes early, the hostess asked me to take the chair just to the left of where K. would be seated. There was a microphone right before

me, as well as one directly in front of David Bohm.*
There was also one before K's chair.

At exactly eleven, K. came into the room and sat
down. Everyone fell silent. K. looked about for a moment and then said, "My, you're all so serious." There
were a few chuckles which lightened the mood.

Immediately K. embarked upon his theme: dependency and how to be free from it. First he went into the
problems of being dependent—the fear and attachments
involved with being dependent on people, things, and
ideas. Then he asked us how we can be free from
dependency on our wives and children, on our friends,
on money, on drink and drugs, on everything that
human beings attach themselves to and become dependent on.

Several people offered their comments, opinions, insights, and understandings. After a while I spoke up. I
said I felt the way to be free from dependency was
through love. I then related an experience I'd had with
my children many years ago. I said that one day I came
to realize how much I humanly loved them and how
much I depended on this love, and that I feared someday something might happen to them which would take
this love away. I said that this wasn't an ongoing fear
but one which would come and go.

I then went on to say that one night when my fear
was quite severe, I realized something needed to be
done. The time had come to examine deeply these feelings. As I did I began to realize the selfishness of my
position; my love was a selfish love and therefore bound

---

*Professor of Theoretical Physics at Birkbeck College, London
University; author of many books including *Wholeness and the Im-
plicate Order* and *The Ending of Time: J. Krishnamurti and Dr.
David Bohm.*

to cause hurt and anxiety and dependency, not only for myself but for my children. When I deeply saw this truth, then I was able to release my self-centered human feelings and begin to love them with a deeper love; I was able to love them with a selfless love. From this selfless, unconditioned love I found I no longer depended on them for my happiness. I just simply and unconditionally loved them. (I wanted to say I loved them with the love I felt from Spirit, but I realized these words wouldn't be acceptable to the group or to K.)

My story seemed to have some impact. K. acknowledged that "yes, love is the only way to be free of dependency." With this the subject changed to love and how we might know what it means to love.

March 20, 1978

Another meeting with K. This time the discussion centered on knowledge and its effect on the human. His question was: Does knowledge keep us rooted to the past? Again there were some opinions and ideas offered, but K. doesn't like this approach. What he likes is for the person to look at his or her own life to find the answer.

I waited quite a while before I spoke. Then I said that I didn't think it mattered whether we had an encyclopedic mind brim full of knowledge as long as the knowledge didn't interfere with our clarity in dealing with and experiencing life. K. concurred and after making several comments of his own, changed the subject to observing and what it means to see clearly, to see factually and not according to an image or an idea.

After years of experiencing and experimenting with "ways" to feel the energy, I have to say that silencing the mind is not the sole way to be with the energy. There are other ways of dying to self. Also, I don't believe God or Love or Truth is helpless in regard to helping us find him or it. I believe if we sincerely desire—intently desire—to find God then we shall be shown. And what we'll be shown will be beyond all our imaginings and fancies, beyond all our beliefs and wishful-hoping. We'll know that it's God because the experience will be so radically different from anything we've ever known, different from anything our minds have ever conjured up.

Having said this, I must also say that Krishnamurti has been a tremendous help to me over the years. Early on he helped to uncloud my mind and to clear the road in my search by requiring that I ask the question, "What is?" Through this I came to realize how much my early search for the True was a muddled, confused, mystical affair. I had little clarity within myself then, because I believed what the "experts" were saying—the gurus, the mystics, the saints—and filled my mind with their thoughts, their "ways," and their experiences instead of experiencing for myself.

In Summary

A dialogue with myself:

"So what is the teaching you speak about?"

I wouldn't call it a teaching so much as a discovery. The discovery is that there's a totally harmonious energy which one can be in contact with. Our being, when we are participating fully with the new energy, is completely harmonious, loving and perfect. This is heaven, a real heaven. It's a heaven humanity has dreamt about from the beginning, a heaven we can live in while living here on earth.

"Why are most people unaware of this energy?"

Because we live so much in the mind and senses. This harmonious energy has nothing to do with the mind and senses. In fact, they have to die down or be diminished for the energy to be.

"You say that a person can learn to live with this energy constantly. How is this possible?"

Once one is in contact with this energy, one realizes that it can be lived with—it can be experienced in every action that we do. And when we do live with it, our lives become harmonious; they must, because the new energy is absolute harmony. Now when problems arise, which they inevitably do, we can "use," apply, direct the energy to the problem. This is what it means to live with love in a world of matter. That's all the discovery is.

"You say that the energy of the mind and senses is disharmonious. Many people would disagree with you."

Perhaps. But if we look objectively at our lives as we operate from the mind and the senses, which is self-will, then I think we'll find that indeed our lives fall into constant disharmony. And this disharmony occurs primarily, I believe, because we're functioning from a material energy rather than from a spiritual energy.

"Spiritual?"

The word really doesn't matter. What does matter is that if we really desire to live life greatly with immense quantities of harmony, caring, and love, then it's imperative that we take a look at things and find out for ourselves if there's a different way of functioning in the world. Again, for me and others, there is a different way, a harmonious way.

"This all seems so esoteric. Here you're talking about some disincarnate energy that we can be in contact with. Maybe only you and a few others—the elect, so to speak—can be in touch with it."

When you've once experienced this other life, this other energy, then you know that it's for everyone; for you intuit or realize through the experience that it's the essence of everyone's being. Thus, to me there's nothing exclusive about the energy. In fact its very nature, its essence, is universal—universal because it's everywhere, both within us and outside us. At least it feels this way when we're experiencing it.

"You emphasize letting go of the body to be in touch with the energy."

Yes. And I believe it's important to understand why; for when we examine the connection between the body and mind, we find that they are a unitary process. They

171

aren't divided in the sense that they function in-
dependently of each other, even though many of us
assume that they do. This is easily seen when we get em-
barrassed or in a panic. Then we can see how the skin
color, the blood pressure, the heartbeat change. From
these simple examples we can see that the body and
mind are inextricably connected. The body, it appears, is
an extension of the mind.

"Let's assume that you're right. I still don't see why it's
so important to let go of the body to experience the
energy, especially in view of what so many mystics,
saints and gurus have said about silencing the mind."

It's because letting go of the body is the letting go of
the entire physical person—that entity which is at enmi-
ty with the spiritual being of the person. It's evident,
too, that the physical person is contained entirely within
his body; mental activities, emotions, sensations—
everything that constitutes this person—is found within
the body. So by letting go of the body we've affected
the entire person. We have put him or her into a state of
suspension which is a temporary death for the human
processes.

Now with the person in suspension and somewhat
dead to self, our awareness and feeling of the energy is
much easier to discern; there's less working for it and
more realizing it, which is unlike our efforts to silence
the mind. This is not to say that the energy won't be experienced when the mind is silent. Most of the time it
will, for when the mind is silent the body is silent and
out of the way. Also with the silencing of the mind a
form of death occurs which naturally opens the person
to this other dimension of life.

"It seems that letting go of the body to attain this new
dimension, this new energy, would be self-centered on
our part and thus defeat our efforts."

Humility, in the sense of letting go of our matter self, is essential to feel this new, harmonious energy. Humility is really a form of death to the self with all its strivings and wants. The self must in some way diminish and end for this other energy to be felt and to stay with us. This is understandable when we realize that the two energies are incompatible; when the one is, the other, to a large extent, isn't.

"Will our minds, which keep us so agitated so much of the time, become silent when we feel this new energy?"

Certainly our minds will be much quieter than they were when functioning from material energy which is agitation in itself. We will find, however, that we don't have to have minds that are totally silent for the energy to be with us. In fact we'll find that the energy can govern our minds and guide our thoughts into areas of activity and creativity; for the energy is Action and Creation.

"Can we come to live with this energy constantly?"

Yes. All it takes is remembering to keep oneself yielded to it.

EPILOGUE

The valley below is located between mountains whose peaks reach up to touch the morning clouds. Its solitude creates an encouragement for one to seek out Spirit deeply. And this is what happened last evening as the darkness was covering all the earth.

I had taken a long walk alone and with each step I let go of everything—the body, thought, my human be-ingness. With the emptying of the unreal, the Real began to fill me. More and more, the fullness of Spirit grew until that was all I was: an entity of Spirit. Now I was walking with the energy of Spirit. Spirit permeated every part of my being and went beyond. It went out into nature and into infinity to return again. Spirit's infinitude was complete, whole, everything and every-where. Its realness was so far beyond matter's dream that it seemed ridiculous that I could ever again feel or live without this fullness.

Now this morning as I write this I once more feel matter's life. But I am encouraged to destroy these feelings so that today will be in the fullness of Spirit as was last night.

Here are more Quest books on holistic healing—

The Healing Energies of Music
By Hal Lingerman
A reference work listing musical compositions suitable for
physical, emotional, and mental therapy.

Health: A Holistic Approach
By Dennis Chernin and Gregory Manteuffel
Two homeopathic physicians focus on nutrition, yoga, stress-
therapy, and homeopathy as therapeutic tools.

Imagineering for Health
By Serge King
Self-healing through the use of the mind.

Healers and the Healing Process
Ed. & Comp. by George W. Meek
Professional medical people investigate the healing methods of the
world's greatest paranormal healers.

I Send a Voice
By Evelyn Eaton
Healings inside of an Indian sweat-lodge.

The Path of Healing
By H. K. Challoner
Spiritual healings based upon the holistic principle present
in all life.

Available from:
Quest Books
306 West Geneva Road
Wheaton, IL 60189